ORKS

DAKKA DAKKA DAKKA,
WAAAAAAGH!

CONTENTS

INTRODUCTION......................3

THE BARBAROUS HORDES.................6

The Green Menace 8
Greenskin Expansion 10
Greenskin Kultur 12
Ork Glyphs 15
Tribes & Clans 16
Gathering the Waaagh! 24
Waaagh! Grukk 26
Warbands of Waaagh! Grukk 28
Split-grin Bad Moons 30
Waaagh! Ghazghkull 32
The Green Tide 34
Da Great Waaagh! 37

ORK WARBANDS.................40

FORCES OF THE ORKS.................52

Orks Wargear List 53
Warboss 54
Weirdboy 55
Mek 56
Big Mek 57
Painboy 58
Mad Dok Grotsnik 59
Kaptin Badrukk 60
Boss Zagstruk 61
Boyz 62
Gretchin 63
Burna Boyz 64
Tankbustas 65
Nobz 66
Meganobz 67
Kommandos 68

FORCES OF THE ORKS (CONTINUED)

Boss Snikrot 69
Trukk 70
Stormboyz 71
Deffkoptas 72
Dakkajet 73
Burna-bommer 74
Blitza-bommer 75
Warbikers 76
Warbuggies 77
Mek Gunz 78
Battlewagon 79
Deff Dread 80
Killa Kans 81
Gorkanaut 82
Morkanaut 83
Lootas 84
Flash Gitz 85
Ghazghkull Thraka 86
Stompa 87
Ork Warband 88

APPENDIX.................92

Warlord Traits 92
Melee Weapons 93
Ranged Weapons 94
Runts & Squigs 97
Orky Know-wots 98
Armour 99
Ork Vehicle Equipment 99
Gifts of Gork and Mork 100
Power of the Waaagh! 101
Ork Horde Detachment 102
Ork Tactical Objectives 103
Reference 104

PRODUCED BY THE GAMES WORKSHOP DESIGN STUDIO

UK	**NORTHERN EUROPE**	**NORTH AMERICA**	**AUSTRALIA**
Games Workshop Ltd,	Games Workshop Ltd,	Games Workshop Inc,	Games Workshop,
Willow Rd, Lenton,	Willow Rd, Lenton,	6211 East Holmes Road,	23 Liverpool Street,
Nottingham,	Nottingham,	Memphis,	Ingleburn,
NG7 2WS	NG7 2WS	Tennessee 38141	NSW 2565

INTRODUCTION

Orks live for battle, and want nothing more than to fight and to kill. Their resilience and belligerence are all but unmatched by the other races of the galaxy, and their immeasurable numbers threaten to crush all who stand against them.

The Orks are formidable enemies to face in battle, each a brutal, simplistic and highly aggressive warrior. For these barbaric monsters, war is its own reward. They believe above all that might makes right, and will fight whoever and whatever they have to in order to prove it. Their ultra violent sense of humour and incredible tolerance for injury mean that death and loss are almost meaningless concepts to the Orks. Most greenskins think little about the future, and are content to fight, eat and steal what they want, then fight some more. Yet when an especially powerful Warboss rises up from the hordes to command the tribes, the Orks are driven into a frenzy of conquest that can consume the stars in a green tidal wave of violence and destruction – a terrifying Ork Waaagh! that few in its path will survive.

WARHAMMER 40,000

If you are reading this codex, then you have already taken your first steps into the Warhammer 40,000 hobby.
Warhammer 40,000: The Rules *contains all the rules you need to fight battles with your Citadel miniatures, and every army has its own codex that acts as a definitive guide to collecting and unleashing it upon the tabletop battlefields of the Warhammer 40,000 universe. This codex allows you to turn your collection of Orks into a mighty horde that will stomp your foes into red ruin.*

ORKS

Ork armies are anarchic, barbaric throngs whose numbers and variety are mind-boggling. Swarming hordes of Orks and grots pour toward the foe alongside clanking, smoke-belching armoured tanks and walkers. The sky is filled with roaring aircraft, while ramshackle convoys of bikes and buggies hurtle off ahead, desperate to be first into the fight. Bizarre artillery fires whistling shells and blasts of energy, while weird inventions flash and buzz. The Orks are a deadly and unpredictable force, so get ready for the Waaagh!.

HOW THIS CODEX WORKS

Codex: Orks contains everything you need to collect your very own greenskin horde and lead it to victory in your games of Warhammer 40,000.

Within these pages you will find the definitive guide to Orks, their violent history and nefarious empires, and the many, many wars they have unleashed upon the galaxy. You will also find a showcase of beautifully painted Ork miniatures exhibiting all the brutal ferocity of their murderous race. Finally, you will also find a full description of each Ork unit, the rules for its use, and an army list that enables you to organise your collection of Citadel miniatures into an army worthy of the mightiest Warboss. Gork and Mork are waiting to be impressed, so get the Boyz together and get ready to fight!

THE BARBAROUS HORDES

Greenskins are one of the most dangerous alien races to plague the galaxy. Numerous beyond belief and driven always to fight and conquer, the greenskins threaten every single race in the galaxy.

Orks are possibly the most warlike aliens in the 41st Millennium, and their number is beyond counting. Amid constant, seething tides of war and bloodshed, burgeoning Ork empires rise and fall. Mercifully most are short-lived, soon destroying themselves in a maelstrom of violence, but should the Orks ever truly unify, they would crush all opposition. The Orks' unquenchable thirst for battle has always proved their downfall: historically, the Ork tribes have spent much of their time fighting amongst themselves, waging brutal wars with only the strongest surviving.

On occasion, an Ork leader will emerge who is mighty enough to defeat his rivals and unite the warring tribes. His success draws other tribes to him, and soon a great Waaagh! is underway – partly a migration, partly a holy war that can exterminate the populations of entire star systems. When the Orks are on the rampage, the galaxy trembles, and in these dark days there are more Waaaghs! rising than ever before.

THE ORK

Orks have but one philosophy: might makes right. They believe that the weak must suffer the rule of the strong. Over the countless millennia in which the greenskins have waged their wars, not one Ork has ever doubted this for a single moment. This unshakeable self-belief is perhaps the most dangerous quality of the Orks, for they will never give up until they plunge the galaxy into an eternal war.

The Orks rule their barbaric civilization with an iron fist. Ugly and violent creatures, they are the dominant life form of a race that includes the smaller Gretchin and Snotling sub-species. Orks see themselves as the toughest race in the galaxy, mightier by far than humans, Eldar or Tau. To prove their point, the Orks are more than willing to fight and kill everything that crosses their path.

Orkoid physique itself is so robust that it can withstand tremendous punishment. They feel surprisingly little pain, even from the most grievous of wounds, enabling them to fight on whilst horrifically injured and even for a short while after being technically dead. It is believed by some who study these brutes, albeit from afar, that this goes some way to explaining the greenskins' ultra-violent sense of humour. As pain and fear mean little to them, they are highly curious and amused by the reactions of their weaker foes as they hack them apart, the screams of terror contrasting with a deep throaty rumbling that, on occasion, could be mistaken for laughter from the Orks and their snickering brethren.

The greenskin regenerative process itself is so powerful that an Ork who has been hacked to bits can simply be stitched back together, bewildered but ready to fight once more. Nothing but the most grievous wounds will put an Ork down for long, and burning them to ash is reputed to be the only way to make absolutely sure that they are gone for good.

A typical Ork stands around the same height as a man, though he would be much taller were he to stand up straight instead of being hunched over, as is his normal stance, and his frame is extremely muscular and solid. An Ork's arms are long and heavily thewed, knuckles almost scraping the floor as he lopes around, and his gnarled hands end in taloned fingers capable of tearing an enemy's throat out with ease.

The skin of an Ork is green and leather-tough, and his body is dotted with scars, scabs, pock-marks and parasites. His skull is extremely thick, able to absorb impacts that would cave in a human head. His heavy brow shades blood-red eyes, afire with the need to kill. Jagged fangs jut from a heavy jaw that would not look out of place upon a far larger predator, and when an Ork speaks, it is in a slow, gruff tone thick with saliva and guttural curses. His words are sparse, brutal and straight to the point.

THE LOST RACE

Many of the more civilised races of the galaxy speculate about where the seemingly omnipresent Ork race came from. Ork legend is generally passed down by the Runtherds, those who specialise in the breeding and training of Gretchin, Snotlings and other squiggly beasts. They speak of a legendary caste of greenskins who created the Orks of today as a warrior race to protect their own. Difficult as it is to believe, this ancient race was supposedly very intelligent, and held dominion over the other greenskins. They were said to be much smaller than their servants, and bred the Orks to be as strong and fierce as possible to protect them from predators and invaders. These mysterious figures, named as Brainboyz in some of the few Ork legends that exist, are said to have developed amazing technologies and directed the greenskins in their expansion across the stars. A great tragedy must have befallen them, however, for they do not exist today (if they ever did). Some Ork legends tell of a great plague that lasted for many centuries, causing the Brainboyz to die out or devolve. Others fondly imagine that they were even more warlike than their servants. These staunch believers violently assert that the Brainboyz took the biggest and best Orks going and set off to find the ultimate war. Perhaps they're out there still, fighting somewhere beyond the stars.

Whatever the truth, the Runtherds tell of how the Brainboyz took steps to preserve what they could of their knowledge. It is said that they used strange sciences to engineer pure knowledge into the bodies and minds of their slaves. Many amongst the Magos Biologis of the Imperium theorise that this is how the Orks retain such a relatively high level of technology, their technical skills hardwired into their genes. Whether or not the legends of the Runtherds or the theories of the Imperium contain a kernel of truth is largely irrelevant in any case. The Orks – though ignorant and brutish – are born survivors. They are resourceful and resilient in the extreme, and they couldn't care less how they got that way.

THE SIMPLE LIFE

One of the greatest strengths the Orks possess is the simplicity with which they approach their existence. For an Ork, the universe is an incredibly straightforward place, free of the angst and worry that plagues most other races. Orks don't try to influence their own destiny and get frustrated when plans don't work out as expected. They don't look for something to blame (except perhaps the nearest Gretchin or a hated rival tribe) and certainly do not reflect on weaknesses in their own way of doing things. They just try again a different way, usually because they have forgotten how they did it the last time. Thus the Orks make remarkable progress by trial and error, without counting the cost. Meanwhile other races steeped in high-flown philosophy fall into the same traps time and again, doomed to stagnate and decline, unless of course they are first conquered by the Orks.

So long as the average Ork has someone to fight, someone bigger than him to tell him who to kill next, and someone smaller than him to beat up, he will know contentment. Orks don't tend to go hungry as they can eat virtually anything, even grots, Snotlings or one another at a pinch. Greenskins have no concept of cannibalism or the moral outrage that accompanies it, as it is only natural that the bigger Orks should live at the cost of those weaker than themselves. With war and killing as their only real motivators, most Orks have little interest in gathering material wealth or luxuries. The one exception to this is a desire to possess ever bigger and louder weapons and vehicles. An Ork will go to almost any lengths to get his hands on a louder shoota or faster buggy. He will obsess over its acquisition until the exact moment he has it, at which point his eye will stray to something even bigger...

In greenskin society, teeth are used as money and form the entire basis of the Ork economy. The teeth, or 'teef', must be big, sharp, ivory-like fangs to have any value – those of races such as humans or the Eldar are just too fiddly and pathetic to have any real worth. The Orks have used teeth as money since time immemorial. It is a natural form of currency, which is particularly useful as Orks shed and replace their teeth every few years. This means that the number of teeth in circulation never diminishes enough to create a shortage, and that no individual Ork can be reduced to dire poverty for too long. This simple approach to an issue most civilisations agonise about is typical of the pragmatic attitude of the Ork race.

> 'THE ORKS ARE THE PINNACLE OF CREATION. FOR THEM, THE GREAT STRUGGLE IS WON. THEY HAVE EVOLVED A SOCIETY WHICH KNOWS NO STRESS OR ANGST. WHO ARE WE TO JUDGE THEM? WE ELDAR WHO HAVE FAILED, OR THE HUMANS, ON THE ROAD TO RUIN IN THEIR TURN? AND WHY? BECAUSE WE SOUGHT ANSWERS TO QUESTIONS THAT AN ORK WOULDN'T EVEN BOTHER TO ASK! WE SEE A CULTURE THAT IS STRONG AND DESPISE IT AS CRUDE.'
>
> - *Uthan the Perverse, Eldar Philosopher*

THE GREEN MENACE

From pirate enclaves to system-spanning empires, Ork holdings are as varied as they are steeped in violence. When they invade a planet or a star system, greenskins bring with them a belligerent ecosystem that overwhelms each conquered world as surely as the Orks themselves crush its defenders.

Greenskin society and ecology is so robust that it can exist almost anywhere, which is why their settlements have been found scattered to the furthest corners of the galaxy. The Imperium has encountered Orks and their kind living – even prospering – in such extreme environments as toxic death worlds, newborn planets still heaving with volcanic activity, or the depressurised carcasses of abandoned orbital platforms. Ork hordes have been found inhabiting drifting ice floes, or infesting irradiated asteroid fields perilously close to active stars. They have been discovered amid corrosive chemical swamps, on lightless nightmare worlds seething with horrific predators, even in the bombed-out remains of planets subjected to Exterminatus. It is rumoured amid the Imperium's Rogue Traders that there are even Ork enclaves hidden within the Eye of Terror itself, though most dismiss this as the ravings of madmen.

No matter where they are encountered or in what numbers, the greenskins are a deadly threat that will multiply exponentially if left unchecked. In a matter of weeks what began as a small raiding party can swell – as if some by some arcane alchemy – into a roiling, anarchic horde bent upon war and destruction. The other races of the galaxy have many theories regarding how their numbers increase so quickly. These range from spontaneous physical division to the release of windblown spores after death. The notorious Vandermeist theorem even claims that the greenskins inhabit an alternative pocket of reality and simply fall through, fully formed, wherever others of their kind are already at war. While many of these wild suggestions are patently ridiculous, it is certainly the case that where one Ork is encountered, more will never be far away. When combined with their relentlessly warlike nature, and tendency to grow larger and more powerful with every battle they survive, it is easy to see how rampaging Orks can quickly overwhelm a planet's defences. A ragged band of Orks allowed to escape the wreckage of their spacecraft and disappear into a city's underhive will return within weeks as a horde of murderous savages, sweeping all before them in their desire for conquest. Those they do not kill will be enslaved, and that which they do not destroy will be looted. Before long, another world will be conquered by the Orks, its cities reduced to ruins and its populace toiling in chains for their brutal greenskin overlords.

Those who have studied Ork settlements (and survived) have observed that Ork civilisation is hierarchical in the extreme. The life of a greenskin is determined not by rank or birth, but by size and savagery. The largest Orks push around their smaller brethren, who in turn bully the diminutive slave-race known as the Gretchin into doing their bidding. Smaller still are the Snotlings, tiny and simple-minded creatures with little use beyond fungus tending or fetching and carrying. The greenskin sub-races have a symbiotic relationship of sorts; the smaller greenskins perform menial tasks for their Ork overseers in exchange for a measure of protection.

GRETCHIN

Although they possess a similar physiology to the Orks, Gretchin are not as strong or as tough as their larger brethren. To compensate for this the Gretchin possess an abundance of low cunning. Commonly known as grots, Gretchin are even more numerous than Orks. They scurry around the larger greenskins on scrawny legs, and their grasping fingers snatch and steal from the unwary. Gretchin have large, bulbous heads and wide tattered ears that flatten against their bald pates when they are afraid (which is most of the time). Sharp fangs fill their jaws, ever ready to be sunk into the flesh of the weak or infirm, and malice gleams in their eyes whenever there is an opportunity for violence.

The grots' large and protruberant noses give them an excellent sense of smell, their ears afford them a similarly advanced sense of hearing, and their eyesight is acute even in the dark. These traits, combined with a heightened instinct for self-preservation, mean that Gretchin can not only survive but even thrive in a society dominated by vicious predators. Some grots have their survival instinct honed to such a degree that they may possess a rudimentary sixth sense, or are naturally far more fortunate than they have any right to be. The grots improve their chances of survival further by exhibiting a fawning and obsequious nature to their Ork masters. Though braver Gretchin will pull faces and make rude gestures behind the backs of the bigger greenskins, few are stupid enough to risk doing so openly.

Grots are fast learners and quick to spot an opportunity, meaning that many wind up as assistants or servants to more important Orks like Mekboyz or Nobz. Others will simply attempt to stay out of the Orks' way, whole groups of grots fashioning hideouts amid scrap piles or warrens of tunnels too constricted for Orks to squeeze their bulk down. When the time comes to go to war, the grots will be flushed out of these hidey-holes en masse by the gnashing squig hounds of the Runtherds, or a few enthusiastic Burna Boyz.

On his own, a single Gretchin poses little threat to a human-sized adversary. However, if there is one quality the grots have in abundance, it is quantity. On the field of battle the Gretchin advance in great mobs, firing volleys of scavenged ammunition from their poor-quality weapons. They then dive upon the fallen and tear them apart in their scrabbling haste to loot the corpses. Even the most accomplished enemy warriors have found their arrogance punctured when cornered by an entire mob of shrieking grots. They can prove especially dangerous during naval boarding actions, for while their Ork masters tie up a ship's defenders in furious point-blank battles, the wily grots will avoid such bloody fighting like the plague. Instead, knots of Gretchin squirm through air-ducts, sabotage or loot vital machine-components, and overwhelm triage stations full of helpless, wounded combatants. When grots wreck a ship's void shield generatorum, or burst from the ducts to overrun a vital chokepoint mid-battle, the foe learn to respect these nasty little greenskins in a hurry.

SNOTLINGS

Snotlings, or 'snots', look like tiny, immature Gretchin. Their scrawny limbs are too small to bear weapons larger or more complicated than shards of broken glass or chunks of scrap. Lacking the violent tendencies of their larger kin, they make for very poor soldiers indeed, and are predominantly kept as little more than pets for their Ork masters, although they make excellent ammunition for the strange weapon the Orks call the shokk attack gun. Nonetheless the snots do perform a valuable function in Ork society.

Snotlings cultivate the great patches of the fungi that spring up around Ork settlements. In this way the Snotlings provide food, drink and medicine for the rest of the greenskin race. Snotlings also look after the ferocious squiggly beasts that live in the Ork cesspits (known to the Orks as 'the drops'). Their natural affinity with these life forms is far greater than that of other greenskins. Helpfully, this means that in a day only a few dozen Snotling attendants will be devoured alive by their ravenous charges.

The Snotling populations that spring up around Ork settlements are monitored and cultivated by a caste of Orks known as Runtherds. These grizzled and merciless slavers use a variety of methods to bully their charges into a state of anxious obedience, not least of which are the much feared grot-prod and the ferocious squig hound.

SQUIGS

Squigs, or squiggly beasts, are an integral part of the mobile and incredibly aggressive greenskin ecosystem. The squigs eat the refuse of the Orks (not to mention local plants, animals and quite often each other) and the Orks eat the squigs. There are many forms of squig and each variety incorporates many subtypes. Mekboyz squeeze viscous black lubricant from the snouts of oil squigs to keep gears and gubbinz working. Painboyz use mending squigs to stitch wounds shut or suture limbs back in place. Eating squigs, parasite hunting squigs, bag squigs, even rare and bizarre sets of musical squigpipes, all have their uses. Yet perhaps the most infamous squigs are the ravenous face-biters, which the Orks use in the same way humans might use attack dogs. Little more than a snapping, drooling mouth on legs, these ferocious beasties are a sign of status and many an Ork Warlord keeps a pet face-biter squig that dines upon those who have fallen out of favour with him. Other equally sharp-toothed squigs grow and breed in the sprawling cesspits of the Ork settlements, lending an air of unpredictability and excitement to even the briefest trip to the drops.

WILDBOYZ

Though the majority of Orks will never venture far from their tribe, there are those strange few who are driven to explore, compelled to do so even in preference to fighting. Such pioneers will seek out the deepest jungles or most arid deserts, where most creatures would struggle to survive at all. Should they endure and multiply, it is common for these remote Ork tribes to degenerate into savages, sometimes known as Wildboyz. After a time, some of these groups will seek out and return to their parent warband. There they learn about Ork kultur and take their place in the warrior society, exchanging spear and axe for slugga and choppa. However, should the new tribe emerge on a world where their Ork ancestors have been driven off or slain, the Wildboyz will instead develop into a tribe of Feral Orks.

At first, Feral Ork tribes pose little threat to the planet they infest. They are uncivilised, even by the low standards of their Ork brethren, and live by the old ways of hunting and exploring. As the tribe increases in size they breed ever-larger varieties of squig, riding around upon great tusked beasts that vary in size from that of a horse to that of a Baneblade. Exploring the stomping grounds of their predecessors, the Feral Orks soon learn to scavenge weapons and equipment, rejoicing in the noise and destruction they can now cause. Shortly after this discovery the tribe will mobilise for war, whooping and howling as they pour out of the mountains or jungles, charging into the settlements of the unsuspecting enemy and starting the whole cycle of warfare afresh. As the war drags on and the mighty Squiggoths are slain one by one, they will be replaced by looted or salvaged tanks covered in beast fetishes that hark back to the squigs that came before. Eventually the Wildboy enclave will mature into a fully-fledged and technologically capable warband in its own right, only to spawn wandering Wildboyz of its own.

GREENSKIN EXPANSION

The galaxy is vast beyond the imaginings of the most ambitious despot. Yet this does not daunt the Orks as they simply don't think about it. Instead, they plough from one conquest to the next, secure in the knowledge that one day, they will rule it all.

Wherever humans have travelled, they have found Orks. It has been tens of thousands of years since Humanity first encountered them, and in that time Mankind has fought countless bloody wars against these savage aliens, and there is no likelihood that this state of affairs will ever change.

There are numerous Ork empires, each spreading across the galaxy like a noxious green stain, and no system is entirely devoid of their touch. Some theorise that the Orks do not use conventional methods of inter-stellar travel because they follow some deep-seated instinctual plan of galactic conquest, but the truth is far simpler. The greenskins have not mastered the art of space travel because they really do not care where they are going, only that they get to fight whatever is there when they arrive.

DREGRUK AND GATHROG

The empires ruled by the Great Despot of Dregruk and the Arch-Dictator of Gathrog have been at war for decades. Lying to the galactic north of the Eye of Terror, the resolution of their conflict could have major repercussions. Should so vast a tide of Orks unite, the resulting Waaagh! could potentially change the face of the war for the Cadian Gate. Were forces from Abaddon's thirteenth Black Crusade to meet it as they poured into the region, the Despoiler's plans for galactic conquest would be severely disrupted, quite possibly saving the entire galaxy from annihilation.

Yet these two Ork empires could never be persuaded to abandon a perfectly good (and very enjoyable) battle for such a noble and civilised cause. Excepting some miraculous act by Gork (or possibly Mork!), the empires of Dregruk and Gathrog will fight on, blissfully unconcerned as their chance to change the fate of all slips away.

CHARADON

The Ork empire of Charadon is the largest and most long standing of its kind. Controlled by a pyromaniac berserker known as the Arch-Arsonist, Charadon has been the bane of Ultima Segmentum for countless centuries. The Arch-Arsonist counts his victories not by the worlds he has conquered but by those left blazing in his wake. His legendary propensity for leaving even the most well-defended worlds as searing conflagrations has garnered him a sprawling empire of greenskins devoted to his cause.

Each successive Warlord of Charadon takes the title of Arch-Arsonist, lending the persona a kind of immortality. Until recently, the expansion of the empire of Charadon was kept to a minimum by the efforts of Chief Librarian Tigurius and the Space Marines of the Ultramarines Chapter. Yet in the face of the increasing Tyranid threat, their success is beginning to wane. The current Arch-Arsonist has seized his chance to invade Ultramar, swearing that he will reduce Macragge itself to cinders.

CALVERNA

The Arch-Maniac of Calverna rose to power after conquering the forge world of Magnos Majoris, the iron heart of the Calverna system. The wily old Deathskulls Warlord then cemented his power for good by having himself wired into the almighty central processing engine of the forge world, turning himself into the biggest Cybork ever seen. Though this rather drastic step has left the Arch-Maniac all but invincible, the vast data-streams pouring into his tiny brain have also driven him quite mad. So it is that, while the Orks of the Calvernan empire are numerous and well equipped with tanks and guns, their attacks are random and display little in the way of logic or cogent strategy.

SPACE HULKS

The primary mode of interstellar travel for the Ork race is the space hulk. Space hulks are gigantic agglomerations of ancient wrecks, asteroids, ice and interstellar flotsam and jetsam, cast together after millennia of drifting in and out of Warp space. Some are infested with alien life forms, Chaos renegades or even worse horrors, but most are simply ghost ships, plying the void for eternity. Yet tales of greedy scavengers meeting horrible fates aboard space hulks are told throughout the Imperium.

When a space hulk appears in an Ork-held system it is seized by any possible means, including colossal traktor beam arrays, and converted into a huge invasion craft. Mobs of Burna Boyz go in first, directed by Meks to carve up obstructions, cut new tunnels and doorways, and flush out any unwanted beasties that may languish on board. Cavernous launch bays are adapted for innumerable assault craft and millions of Ork warriors and war machines honeycomb its irregular cavities. Once completed, the space hulk is sent back out into the stars with an attendant fleet of attack ships and kroozers as escorts. The space hulk is guided into a Warp storm or rift through the efforts of its Weirdboyz and Meks. It is drawn into the Immaterium and, if all goes well, spat out once more at a world ripe for conquest.

Being incredibly random in their trajectory, space hulks could appear in any place, at any time. This suits the Orks just fine, as their spirit of adventure and aggression owes nothing to organisation or direction. In this way the Orks travel the galaxy, spreading a plague of warfare across space and time.

DISTRIBUTION OF PRIMARY ORK ENCLAVES

The schematic below shows the current major concentrations of Orkoid presence in the charted galaxy.
Active Waaaghs! are shown with directional arrows to denote the prevailing paths of the conquest thus far.

KEY

- High Levels of Ork Infestation
- Active Waaagh!
- Forge World
- Astra Militarum World
- Space Marine World
- Knight World
- Misc Location

THE GHOUL STARS

WAAAGH! BORK

THE GRAND WARLORD

Desperation

Taurabrax

Avarris

Triplex Phall

THE EASTERN FRINGE

Angelis

Dragon's End

ULTIMA SEGMENTUM

GREAT TYRANT OF JAGGA

Attila

TAU EMPIRE

CHARADON SECTOR

Agrellan

THE REALM OF ULTRAMAR

Canto II

ARCH-KILLA OF CHRISIOS

Incaladion

Accatran

Metalica

Ichar IV

Macragge

WAAAGH! GORBAD

Bal (Blood Angels)

Hephastine

Kolossi

ARCH-ARSONIST OF CHARADON

Valhalla

WAAAGH! GHAZGHKULL

WAAAGH! NAZDREG

THE MAELSTROM

Estaban System

GOTHIC SECTOR

Molech

WAAAGH! URGOK

Chocoris

Rynn's World

GREAT DESPOT OF DREGRUK

Goth

Ryza

Badab

HALO STARS

Mordian

Alaric

Catachan

Octaria

Nocturne

Adransa Cluster

SEGMENTUM TEMPESTUS

ARCH-DICTATOR OF GATHROG

Cypra Mundi

Styken System

Fenris

Lyrithor

ARMAGEDDON

Kantarak Sector

Necromunda

Deliverance

Cadia

SEGMENTUM SOLAR

Terra

ARCH-MANIAC OF CALVERNA

Tallarn

THE VEILED REGION

THE EYE OF TERROR

Medusa

Stygies

Krieg

Graia

Artemia Majoris

WAAAGH! WAZDAKKA

SEGMENTUM PACIFICUS

Ultima Macharia

GREENSKIN KULTUR

The Ork way of life is as straightforward and brutal as the Orks themselves. Much like their approach to everything else, Orks do not waste time pondering why they do things, or how they might do them better. Instead they simply act, instinct and ability driving them on in a never-ending cycle of violence and conquest.

Orks have their own distinct culture (or 'kultur' as the Orks call it), the origins of which are lost in the dim and distant past. Though likely a corruption of whatever may have come before, by and large it functions very well. Perhaps this is because the fundamental tenet of their society is a simple one that even the most pea-brained Snotling can understand – might makes right.

THE ORK HIERARCHY

Orks instinctively obey those larger than themselves, provided they are a healthy shade of green – most Orks would rather die than bow to a non-greenskin's will. The rulers of Ork society are the most powerful Orks of all, known as Warbosses or Warlords. These monstrous killing machines can reach up to ten feet in height, and their sheer muscular bulk makes them wider at the shoulder than a fully armoured Space Marine. Though some Warbosses rise to prominence through low cunning, most seize power through the application of brute force. A Warboss will hold dominion over all he surveys, and beat the living daylights out of anyone who says different. His decisions are enforced

by a ruling caste of Orks known as Nobz, who are larger, richer and more aggressive than normal Orks, and never miss an opportunity to remind them of it.

The bulk of an Ork horde, which can be hundreds or even thousands strong, is comprised of great mobs of infantry that call themselves Boyz. Goff mobs in particular are famous for the sheer number of Boyz that they can field at war, often outnumbering their foes several times over.

Orks tend to be lazy and forgetful, and only war and the preparations beforehand really bring out their innate talents. Though the bigger, meaner Ork Boyz will lord it over the smaller, ganglier ones, even a subservient Ork is of limited use when it comes to practical tasks that don't involve fighting. Most of the day-to-day running of Ork society is therefore left to the Gretchin, whose duties include preparing food, taking messages, hauling stuff about, general organisation and just being around the place when an Ork wants something to kick. This gives the Orks plenty of time to swagger about, getting into fights and coming up with new ways to kill things.

The Gretchin are happy enough in their role. They bear little resentment towards their superiors, for to them Orks are just a fact of life. Questioning this usually leads to a clip round the ear, and not much else. Individual Gretchin can enjoy a relatively comfortable existence by providing valuable services to their Ork masters. In fact the Gretchin have created an entire enterprise culture of their own within their Ork-dominated society, and many Gretchin operate their own black market businesses on the side, selling fungus beer, roasting squigs on sticks, coordinating the bets when a fight breaks out and then looting the resulting corpses.

A LIFE OF CONFLICT

Orks excel in the field of war, on everything from a personal to a galactic scale. Conflict governs their entire society, their technological advances, and even their individual growth. Prolonged periods of conflict lead to a proportional increase in the size and strength of an Ork, and greenskins who have fought in an active warzone for a few years tower over those deprived of such stimulus: longer wars produce ever-larger combatants. At the climax of Warlord Thogza's decades-long Waaagh! into the Duros sector, many of the Ork veterans were reputed to have grown to almost twice as tall as a man.

When there are no enemies to fight the Orks will test their mettle against any native predators they can find, and if that fails they will fight amongst themselves simply for the joy of it. Disputes between Orks become almost hourly occurrences if they are not engaged against a common foe. It is during such times that a Warboss' authority may be challenged by rival Nobz. Such power struggles are resolved through methods ranging from low cunning to high explosives, but ritual pit fighting remains a firm favourite. Pit fights are popular since they entertain the whole warband and establish the victor as Warboss beyond dispute. Either rivals are dispatched by the incumbent Warboss, or he is overthrown (and usually killed into the bargain). Every Ork settlement has a fighting pit for this purpose, which is also used to settle other grudges and disputes. Pit fighting thus serves the Orks as a rough and ready judicial system.

Other tests of mettle popular in Ork kultur are squig-eating contests, whereby rival Orks attempt to eat a face-biter squig before it eats them, and breakneck races around the settlement's perimeter in rickety vehicles. It is generally frowned upon to open fire upon a challenger in a race such as this, or at least during the first lap.

As an Ork matures into adulthood, he will become involved in larger and more violent conflicts ranging from border skirmishes to all-out war. Orks fixate upon things they enjoy, and the heightened states of excitement they experience during battles can mean that over the course of a particularly epic conflict an Ork will become addicted to one facet of warfare above all others. Like-minded tribemates who share the same obsessions will often seek each other out, forming loose groups of specialists. An Ork who has experienced the exultation of destroying an enemy tank or walker may join the ranks of the Tankbustas, whereas an Ork who just can't stop setting things on fire will soon start hanging around with the local Burna Boyz. However, the largest and most popular of all of these subcultures is the Kult of Speed.

THE KULT OF SPEED

Orks love to go fast. There is something about speed that fulfils some deep need in the Orkish temperament, just like the thunder of guns, the clank of tracks or the din of battle. They like to feel the wind whipping into their faces and to hear the throaty roar of supercharged engines. It is hardly surprising that bikes and buggies of all kinds are popular with the Orks. These up-gunned vehicles may not be as sturdy as those used by the Imperium, but they are cheap, can pack a massive amount of firepower and, most important of all, they can achieve truly suicidal speeds.

Those Orks who become addicted to the sensation of speed will most likely find their way into the Speed Freeks, a kult whose members rarely if ever leave the saddle. These grinning loons roar into battle on exhaust-belching jalopies and crude but effective flying machines, intent on getting into the thick of the fighting before their ground-pounding comrades. Due to the large number of vehicles in each warband, they often have several of the Oddboyz known as Meks amongst their number to keep their vehicles running.

MADBOYZ

Madboyz are those Orks whose minds didn't develop quite right, or who have taken a chunk of shrapnel to the brain. Though they are physically identical to other Orks, the fact they wear outlandish garb and carry everything from rusty buckets to stuffed squigs into battle proves that they are very different in all sorts of entertaining ways.

Madboyz often form informal retinues for Weirdboyz, and live apart from other Orks in small shanty towns. Mobs of Madboyz are considered to be lucky, their presence a sign of good fortune. However, this does entail a degree of inconvenience, such as when they decide to hold impromptu shouting contests in the middle of a night raid, or pelt the foe with a volley of stikkbomb pins before waiting expectantly for the loud bangs to start.

The fact remains that Madboyz are a surprisingly potent asset on the battlefield, for their antics often confound the foe. Even the most gifted tactician cannot predict the anarchic movements of a mob of Madboyz caught up in the excitement of battle. After all, how can you second-guess an enemy who is as likely to tear apart an infantry platoon with their bare hands as they are to mill about picking snot-grubs out of each others' noses?

ODDBOYZ

If Orks were just single-minded killing machines they would be dangerous enough, but they would be unable to sustain the level of technology required to ply the stars. Gretchin, though obedient if beaten with sufficient regularity, are not inventive enough to maintain the weaponry that the Orks possess, nor to patch up casualties when the going gets tough. These highly technical demands are met by a caste of Orks known as Oddboyz.

There are many types of Oddboy in Ork society, but the most important are Mekboyz, Painboyz, Runtherds and Weirdboyz. Mekboyz are responsible for the creation and maintenance of Ork technology. Painboyz are Ork medics, though their penchant for bizarre and inappropriate surgery can make their ministrations more hazard than help. Runtherds breed the lesser forms of greenskin and marshal them on the field of battle, and Weirdboyz are potent psykers who can discharge great blasts of Waaagh! energy, the psychic power subconciously generated by greenskins, particularly during battle, into the ranks of the foe.

Although it may seem strange to humans, these Oddboyz all possess an innate understanding of their fields of expertise without having to be taught. A Mekboy knows how to create engines and generators even though he has never been taught to do so, and a Painboy instinctively knows which squirty tube connects to which wriggly bit when he is delving into some unfortunate patient's abdomen. If asked where this knowledge comes from an Oddboy might reply that it was in his blood all along.

It seems possible that the abilities of Orks to build machines, practise medicine or even use psychic powers are passed down through Ork society on a primordial, biological level. No studies of the greenskins have ever successfully determined how this process works. Yet it seems most likely that the knowledge is hardwired into the very cellular make-up of the Orks, perhaps a legacy left to them by their legendary Brainboyz. However he comes by his latent knowledge, as an Ork matures it will start to make itself apparent, leading him to assume the role in Ork society for which he is best suited. Should he lack any specialist knowledge, the Ork will happily join the vast throng of Boyz at the heart of each tribe and content himself with a life of murder and mayhem.

THE NATURE OF THE BEAST

Theories abound that Orks harbour the genetic traits of both animal and fungal life forms, and that it is this unusual biology that gives an Ork his remarkable constitution. Orks' green colouration could be explained, scholars suggest, due to some form of algae that permeates their cellular makeup. Such a substance could break down and repair damaged tissue at an incredible rate, accounting in part for the Orks' extremely durable metabolism. Those observers of other races who maintain this theory point to the fact that an Ork's head can live for some time after being completely severed from the body. Indeed, operations to reattach these are a staple of many a Painboy's repertoire (staple being the operative word!).

Yet for all the questions that hang over the greenskin race, what cannot be disputed is its relentlessly bloodthirsty nature. An invasion by Orks has been likened to an incurable disease by the Imperium's scholars. Once a world or system has faced attack by the greenskins once, it will be ravaged by them time and again until it finally withers and dies. Even as a world's defenders are celebrating their first victory over the Ork invaders, new tribes of greenskins will be multiplying in the dark and shadowed corners of the victorious world. At the same time, Ork survivors will carry word with them through the void, spreading the tale of how good a fight a particular world put up. Keen to have a go themselves, fresh waves of Orks will soon descend upon the horrified defenders, often before the damage from the previous Ork incursion has been put straight. These attacks will increase in severity, wave after wave of greenskins from

space now supplemented by the tribes that have risen up from the world's wilderness. The planet's populace will be overrun one stronghold at a time, drowning in a rising tide of roaring, battle-mad greenskins.

The harder a planet's defenders fight back, the worse their predicament will become. Every Ork slain makes way for two of its bellowing brethren, while every attack wave the defenders bloodily repulse just draws more enthusiastic greenskins down on their heads. In this way some worlds can become the unintentional focus of a Waaagh!, the Orks' numbers and frenzy reaching critical mass as they fling themselves against the world's defences time and again. Eventually the pressure from Ork invaders both within and without becomes insupportable, leaving the defenders only two choices: stand and fight, dying to the last in the process, or flee with whatever they can salvage, leaving their stricken world to the Orks.

THE ORK GODS

The Orks are a powerful force in the universe. A highly prolific race, they are able to expand and prosper effortlessly in comparison to the other civilisations who struggle even for simple survival. The Ork character traits have a reflection in the Warp just like the impulses and emotions of Humanity and the Eldar. These traits are made manifest in the belligerent Ork gods known as Gork and Mork.

The Orks say that Gork is brutal but kunnin', and Mork is kunnin' but brutal. Gork and Mork are divine powerhouses, deities so strong they are never truly defeated. They simply shrug off the attacks of other gods with a raucous laugh. Gork grins, bares his long teeth, and lands a mighty blow on his adversary's head with a spiked club the size of a comet. Mork, always the sneaky one, waits until his foe isn't looking before clobbering him with a low blow.

An idea of the appearance of the Ork gods can be gained from looking at Ork Gargants and Stompas, mighty war machines constructed in the image of Gork (or possibly Mork). The Mekboyz create these titanic engines of war to reflect the essence of Orkiness in mechanical form, and as such they serve as potent religious idols. To the Orks, these clanking behemoths behave very much like their gods, lumbering about and leaving a trail of devastation in their wake. They go where they please, and never shun a fight.

The aspects of Gork and Mork are likewise evoked by the Gorkanaut and Morkanaut. These huge armoured war suits are intended as a tribute to and imitation of their chosen god all in one, and their pilots are frequently gripped by visions of Gork (or possibly Mork) urging them on during the heat of battle.

As the apocalyptic designs of the Chaos Gods approach fruition, the immaterial realm is roused to ever greater fury. So it is that Gork and Mork fight all the harder against the daemonic tides washing about their feet. The Ork gods' joyful battle-lust echoes into the material universe, their roars clearer to the greenskins with every passing day. The Weirdboyz claim that Gork and Mork are calling all their children to the last mighty battle, for the Great Waaagh!, the everlasting war, is upon them.

ORK GLYPHS

The Ork language is written in a form of glyphic script. The core of the script is composed of glyphs that indicate clan, tribe, common Ork concepts and elements of Ork names. This is augmented by phonetic symbols which can be used to write most Ork words, along with any alien names or words.

 Bad: Evil, wicked, strong, tough

 Blitz: Invasion, devastate

 Boss: Leader, officer, head Ork, warlord

 Dakka: Attack, noisy weapon, shoot, fight

 Gul: Death, bones, skull, rocks, white

 Gob: Mouth, eat, drink, speak out of turn

 Gof: Warlike, spiky, metal, black, night

 Gor: Blood, red, slaughter, wound

 Grim: Ruthless, prowess, face, dangerous

 Grod: Friend or favourite enemy

 Grot: Gretchin, servant, slave

 Mek: Clever, technology, mechanical

 Mor: Wild, feral, ancient

 Naz: Moon, shine, light, wealth

 Nob: Nobillity, authority, high rank

 Ordz: Many, loads

 Orky: Ork, Ork kultur, good, green

 Ruk: Attack, charge

 Skraga: 'Ardboy, veteran

 Skul: End of battle, dead

 Snik: Cut, kill, slay, execute, assassinate

 Squig: Squig, food, eat, supplies, useful

 Stomp: Boot, stormboy, drill, march

 Teef: Wealth, tribute

 Tuf: Old, ancient

 Ulk: Space hulk, spaceship, cruiser

 Waaagh: Warband, tribe, watch out!

 Warp: Space, the Warp

 Wazza: Speed, Kult of Speed

 Wurr: Weird, strange

 Zag: Lightning, movement, fast strike

 Zog: Go away, get lost, no good

A	F	K, C or Q	Nt	S	Uz	0
Ag	G	L	O	Sh	V	1
Ar	Ga	M	Og	Sk	W	2
B	Go	Ma	Ork	Sn	Wa	3
D	Gr	Mo	Ot	T or Th	Y	4
Du	Gu	N	P	Ug or Uk	Z or Az	5
E, Ee or I	H	Na	R	Ur	Zu	Lotz

TRIBES & CLANS

The Orks are an incredibly anarchic race. Their armies and settlements seem utterly disorganised to outside eyes. Yet in truth Ork society is governed by a rugged set of tried and tested traditions that no greenskin would ever consider changing.

Orks thrive on conflict. The strongest rise to the top while the weak become subservient and benefit from the superior leadership and headkicking skills of their conquerors. To an Ork this state of affairs is perfectly satisfactory. If an Ork tribe is beaten by another, stronger tribe, the defeated Orks welcome the opportunity to be led into battle by a new Warlord of even greater power.

A tribe is simply all the Orks in a given location, regardless of what kult or clan they may belong to, because in the end an Ork is an Ork and they will always put aside their differences if there is an opportunity to attack a common foe. Each tribe is led by a Warlord whose authority and power holds this loose confederation in check and prevents civil war between the rival elements of the tribe. Tribes can vary in size from a few hundred Orks to a few million, depending on the influence of the war leader at the top of the pile.

Because a Warlord cannot be everywhere at once, the tribes are split into warbands that in turn are led by factional leaders called Warbosses. Each Warboss leads a warband of a hundred or so Orks, forming a rough and ready army that is capable of taking on almost any foe. Most warbands have a hard core of Ork infantry at their heart, but beyond this they vary enormously from one to the next. Like-minded Orks tend to cluster together, leading to warbands crammed with mechanised Speed Freeks or pyromaniac Burna Boyz. The Warboss' preferences can also dictate how their warband looks and fights, some favouring masses of charging Boyz and hulking Nobz, while others prefer to ride to battle aboard columns of ragged armoured vehicles, or packing batteries of massive shootas and artillery.

Although all Orks belong to a tribe, most also belong to clans such as the Goffs or Evil Sunz. Tribes are constantly breaking apart and reforming in the crucible of battle, but the clans are constant and enduring. A large tribe usually contains many different clans, and each clan has its own distinct character and identity. There are six clans in particular that have spread from one side of the galaxy to the other: the Goffs, the Snakebites, the Bad Moons, the Blood Axes, the Deathskulls and the Evil Sunz. Most warbands will contain representatives of at least one of these clans, each of which has distinct cultural preferences, traits and strengths.

GOFFS

A Goff likes nothing more than hearing the hammering of guns and that satisfying wet crunch when his choppa finds its way deep into the throat or chest of an enemy. They will seize upon any excuse to start a brawl, even amongst themselves and often all it takes is a misinterpreted glance in their general direction or grunted insult to start the fists flying, the Boyz quickly forgetting the reason for the bust-up and simply enjoying the resulting fight. This preference for near-constant scrapping amongst themselves also serves a practical purpose between battles, keeping them honed as specialists in hand-to-hand combat, as they prefer to wage their wars up close and personal.

Goff-dominated warbands are notorious for the sheer number of Ork infantry they muster in times of war. All it takes is the hint of a good fight and the Goffs appear in droves, flocking to any Warboss who can promise them the chance of opening some skulls. Because of their preference for close combat, Goffs prefer to fight on foot, usually only hitching a lift on passing Trukks so they can jump off nearer to the enemy and get stuck into them as soon as possible.

Goff mobs are usually dozens strong, and a true Goff horde has multitudes of Boyz at its heart, so that when the Goffs go to war, the ground shakes to a stampeding thunder of steel-capped boots. Enemies often interpret these horde tactics as a means to overwhelm set defences and soak up casualties during an assault. More likely though each individual Goff is just following the rest of their mob, rightly reasoning that if an Ork is charging across the battlefield there will be something to attack at the other end.

The Goffs use a bull's head as their clan emblem, as they feel a kinship with bad-tempered, violent and flatulent beasts. Horned helms are also seen as a symbol of the clan's aggression, and can even make handy weapons, making a head butt or head-first charge even more vicious. They dress predominantly in black, on the basis that dressing up in flashy colours 'is fer wimps and Madboyz'. Though they sometimes decorate their wargear with checks and dags, Goffs are disgusted by the concept of camouflage. Not only do the Goffs consider the idea of deliberately hiding from a fight cowardly, but they also cannot comprehend why an Ork might not want to 'have a go'.

They view all the other clans as inferior, with most Goffs seeing it as their Gork-given right to lord it over the other Boyz. For this reason a lot of Warbosses and Nobz tend to be Goffs, their love of bashing heads making them natural Ork leaders, with a talent for keeping unruly mobs of Boyz in line. Goffs also have a fearsome reputation in the fighting pits. The saying 'a Goff is always worth his teef' comes from how hard they are to beat, it being a well known fact among the tribes that betting teef on a Goff is always a cunning plan. Goffs however consider making teef off fights only a by-product of the fights themselves. As any self-respecting Goff will tell his Boyz, fightin' for teef is one thing, but a proper Goff should always be willing to break faces for free.

GUTRAK DETHHEAD

Warboss Gutrak is an imposing figure, a brutish Goff with a huge bionik klaw and a serrated steel-like skull mask spattered in the dried blood of his most recently defeated foes. When he fought for the Great Tyrant of Jagga, Gutrak gained a brutal reputation as one of the Tyrant's best fighters. However, Gutrak's destiny was to change when his tribe landed on the carrion world of Eclipos. The planets's only settlement was an Adeptus Mechanicus research outpost at its northern polar ice cap. Gutrak and his Boyz struck the outpost like a hammer blow from the sky, their rust ships and roks raining down as the occupants frantically assumed defensive positions. The handful of Tech-Priests and Gun Servitors were no match for the Goffs, the Orks hacking and blasting them apart before searching the underground Adeptus Mechanicus complex for more heads to cave in. It was Gutrak that found the massive door, as high as a Gargant and twice as wide. It looked like the servitors had been trying to seal it up, which only made Gutrak more interested in what might be on the other side. When he heaved it open, the cave beyond gave a great mechanical groan, and thousands upon thousands of pairs of eyes blinked into flickering eerie life. The Goffs could not believe their luck as row upon row of metal men began to march forwards to destroy them. Needing no order to attack, the Boyz charged into the cavern, hacking and smashing them apart, until Gutrak personally broke their leader in half and ripped off his metal face to wear as a mask, taking the name Dethhead in honour of his new trophy. No one knows if it was through some influence of his new alien trophy which lit the fires of ambition within Gutrak, but he left the Jagga Waaagh! after that battle, taking his Boyz with him.

EVIL SUNZ

The Orks belonging to the Evil Sunz clan are irresistibly attracted to every conceivable kind of fast vehicle. Be it low-sprung buggies, monstrous Warbikes, or supersonic aircraft, Evil Sunz will spend every toof they possess in order to own them. The richest Evil Sunz can even afford to have a Mek customise their ride, bolting on more wheels, bigger engines and louder rockets. Anything that looks like it might make the vehicle go faster is fair game, so it is not unusual to see wings attached to Warbikes, jet-engines mounted on the back of Trukks, or even more bizarre means of propulsion such as Squig treadmills and massive propellers.

Should an Evil Sunz Ork live long enough, he will inevitably acquire his own vehicle, whether he buys it with carefully hoarded teef or takes the simpler route of just nicking it from another clan member. If an Evil Sunz Ork cannot drive into battle, he will ride, and if he cannot ride at least he can content himself with being close to the throaty, growling engines of their wagons, his nostrils filled with their satisfying promethium stink. Evil Sunz who therefore have to fight on foot will usually race into battle crammed into Trukks or Battlewagons, or at least run as fast as they can towards the enemy bellowing a throaty battle roar.

The Evil Sunz never stay in one place for long, and are always on the lookout for new victims and settlements to slaughter. Clan members have a tendency to leave a battle midway through if it looks like the main part of the fighting is over, or abandon a burning city or ruined world if there is nothing left worth killing. Evil Sunz especially like a good chase, as it gives them a chance to really open up the throttle on their vehicles. Enemy forces that turn tail on the Evil Sunz often learn this to their misfortune, as the disorganised Orks are suddenly sent into a frenzy as their foes try to race away.

The armies of the Imperium find it extremely difficult to engage the Evil Sunz on anything other than the Orks' terms, for their super-charged speedsters can outmanoeuvre the heavy vehicles of the Imperial Guard with ease. One favoured tactic of Evil Sunz warbands will is to charge into the enemy, only to keep right on charging out the other side so they can wheel around and charge again: long columns of Warbikes, buggies and Trukks making ad hoc cavalry-like attacks, snaking in and out of the enemy while the Orks on board whoop and yell, firing their guns out of windows.

The totem of the Evil Sunz clan is a blood red Ork face grimacing from the heart of a sunburst. They wear red armour and often paint their machines red too, firmly believing in the old Ork adage that 'red ones go fasta', and Evil Sunz Warbosses will usually have their vehicles painted red from grille to exhaust. This habit of painting vehicles red has its roots in the ritual covering of Ork mounts with the blood of the foe, a tradition that is still observed with relish by some Evil Sunz to this day.

JAZGOB'S JET-BOYZ

Jazgob's Jet-Boyz have become a legend among the Evil Sunz for their kustom vehicles. Each of their cherished rides mounts a specially crafted engine under their bonnet, scavenged from the remains of a downed Dakkajet. Jazgob's own ride is a grossly oversized Warbike built around a single massive engine. In battle, he will sit proudly astride the engine, its howling turbine blades making the whole bike buck and kick like a living thing as it hurls the Evil Sunz Ork across the battlefield. Few Evil Sunz could hope to afford such an impressive personal ride, let alone a whole warband's worth of jet-powered wagons. Jazgob came by his wealth not by teef-smashing but rather because he was in the right place at the right time, and like most Evil Sunz was the quickest to get there. Every Evil Sunz warband is always on the lookout for those Meks who can offer to build bigger and better Trukks, bikes or buggies. For this reason Jazgob and his Boyz threw in their lot with Big Mek Cogtoof, having heard of his ambitions to capture the space hulk Starkrumpa. *Smashing aboard in blade-toothed boarding craft, the Orks found the vast hulk was infested with Genestealers, the clawed horrors stirring to life with their arrival. After days of bloody battle, the Orks had wiped out most of the creatures except for the Broodlord and his nest. Cogtoof offered the Ork who brought him the skull of the Genestealer Broodlord anything he wanted. While other Orks mobbed up to charge into the nest, Jazgob and his Boyz raced past them on their bikes, careening off corridor walls and leaving thick trails of exhaust in their wake. Jazgob personally killed the Broodlord, ramming it into the wall with his Warbike before scorching off its face, and claimed a fleet of kustom vehicles from Cogtoof as his reward.*

BAD MOONS

The Bad Moons are the richest of all the Ork clans. This is because their teeth grow faster than anyone else's, meaning that even the lowliest Bad Moon Ork has a steady supply of wealth. This is not regarded as an unfair advantage, as any Ork who is big and ferocious enough can simply smash the teeth out of a Bad Moons' head. In fact, many Ork Warbosses like to keep a mob of Bad Moons around for just this purpose, their toothy gobs a ready supply of extra teef. It's often not a terrible deal for the Bad Moons either, as any Ork tough enough to beat their teeth out of them is usually one worth following into a fight.

The Bad Moons fulfil the role of what passes for a merchant class within Ork society, and if something can be bought or sold, odds are the Bad Moons will have it. Some Runtherds reckon that it must have been the Bad Moons that came up with the whole concept of teef being used to buy things, when the clan figured out how quick their teeth grow. Of course there are other Runtherds who say it is the other way round, and when teef became Ork currency the Bad Moons made their teeth grow quicker so they would have the most. In either case, Orks seldom dwell on such things for long, as knocking out teeth is far more interesting than talking about them.

All this wealth means that Bad Moons have an ostentatious reputation, and their vehicles are festooned with gaudy decoration and gold plating, as is the majority of their wargear. As gold is considered practically worthless by most Orks, being too soft to make good weapons or vehicles, they are more than happy to trade it away to Bad Moons for the more valuable teef. Bad Moons love gold more than any other metal, and will commonly have a couple of glinting teeth in their avaricious grins.

Bad Moons mobs are always well equipped, at least by Ork standards. Their Nobz often sport flashy back banners and massive, kustomised weapons, and are followed by entourages of scurrying grot servants loaded down with ammo and chests of teef. Some of this ornamentation is simply to show other Orks just what a big deal the Bad Moons are. This could include huge coloured totems above their wagons bearing grinning Ork faces, or teetering statues of Gork or Mork built from precious metals and stones all mashed together (they're more valuable that way).

The Bad Moons favour golden yellow and black for their wargear, taking a snarling moon on a field of flames as their clan emblem. Their armour and wargear is painted with gaudy patterns in the clan colours and they have more jewellery and piercings than any other Ork clan. If something looks valuable, a Bad Moon will find a way to wear it, stick it through his body or bolt it onto the side of his vehicle, preferably somewhere that every other Ork can clearly see it. However, it is only a fool who underestimates the raw strength of the Ork underneath the ostentation. A Bad Moons Warboss is just as happy to use a shiny boss-pole to smash skulls in as he is to use it to boast of his wealth.

MOGDOS GILT-TOOF

Said to be the richest Ork in all Charadon, Mogdos' deep coffers of teef are vast enough to pay for the services of the best Big Meks and Painboyz around. Once, he was a mere fang-ripper from a Bad Moons scrap fleet that was following in the shadow of a tendril of Hive Fleet Leviathan. The Ork vessels were scavenging the dead worlds the forward elements of the Tyranids had attacked, before the bio-ships stripped the worlds completely. All was going well until the crews of the scrap fleet disturbed a dormant nest of bio-horrors on a dead human factory world. Mogdos was the only Nob to make it back to the fleet alive after the ensuing battle, and 'inherited' its wealth, setting up base in the nearby Charadon Ork empire and throwing in his lot with the Arch-Arsonist Snagrod. Since then Mogdos has followed Snagrod on his rampage across the Ultima Segmentum, making sure the other Warbosses pay their due and commissioning Meks to build the biggest and best war machines. For this reason the Arch-Arsonist keeps the Bad Moon and his Boyz around, their flashy wagons and Mogdos' golden grin a prominent fixture in the Waaagh!. Mogdos' reputation also extends beyond the reaches of the Charadon empire, and stories tell of how, when he filled his first ship full of teef, he hid most of it. This legend of Gilt-Toof's treasure is told, in the main, by grizzled old Freebooterz, and has inspired many a greedy warband of Orks to wander off into the void looking for it, raiding worlds, and terrorising local populations in their quest for the alleged cave full of teef. However, the Freebooterz' stories contradict each other, each one giving different clues to the planet's location, ensuring the legend of Gilt-Toof's hidden hoard continues to remain a mystery.

SNAKEBITES

Considered backward by the more technologically-minded tribes, Snakebites still follow the old ways. Scorning complicated matters like making their own guns or vehicles, the clan put their faith in things they can trust; a good bit of sharpened bone, a heavy stick or a nice keen-edged choppa. In battle they will daub themselves with mud and crude war-paint, hanging the claws and teeth of beasts they have killed around their necks and wearing poorly cured skins.

As a result of their rugged lifestyle, a Snakebite's appearance is weather-beaten and they are as tough as old boots. They are experts in the field of breeding stock and their grots and squigs are the most genuinely vicious and dangerous in all of Orkdom. When a tribe of Snakebites joins a battle it brings with it a menagerie of these beasts, their camp a chaos of ravaging, snarling squigs and running, screaming grots. When other Orks are looking for an aggressive attack squig or an unusually fierce or obedient grot they come to the Snakebites. Squig-baiting is also a speciality of the Snakebites, and when an Ork is not brawling he will often wander down to the clan's camp to watch a bunch of grots get thrown into a pit with a ravenous giant squig.

The most fearsome beasts bred by the Snakebites though are their mighty Squiggoths: huge, towering creatures capable of knocking over battle tanks and trampling entire platoons. These ornery monsters are reared from particularly ill-tempered young squigs that will quickly progress from biting off fingers and hands to devouring careless grots and anything else that strays into their pens. However, a well trained Squiggoth will become almost completely loyal to its Snakebite master, recognising him by his distinct smell, and reserving its rage for its master's enemies.

The Snakebites clan's name and emblem comes from a rite of passage that involves a young aspirant goading an extremely poisonous serpent into biting them, then sucking out the venom to prove their toughness. This leads Snakebites to build up an immunity to venoms, and they usually bring poisonous serpents to each new world they invade in case the local wildlife proves disappointingly inoffensive. As far as a Snakebite is concerned, snakes make the best pets – obviously, the more aggressive the better.

The Snakebites' Runtherds breed large numbers of Gretchin, who in times of war are given weapons and herded into battle, often manning artillery batteries. Ironically, the more sophisticated weapons that fall into the hands of the Snakebites usually find their way into the hands of their grots, as the runts of the tribe are left to figure out how they work. The Orks, meanwhile, gather into especially large and surly mobs, whose lack of shootas is more than made up for by their assortment of heavy, blunt objects. When the Snakebites launch an assault, it is with such shocking ferocity that the enemy is buried under an avalanche of battle-crazed Orks, snapping squigs and gun-wielding grots. Though they may be rather low-tech, the Snakebites are a deadly foe.

THE WYRM-KILLA TRIBE

When Waaagh! Bork rampaged out of the Ghoul Stars and into the Eastern Fringe, the Wyrm-Killa tribe came with them. Festooned with alien trophies and covered in scars, this Snakebite tribe earned their name killing Tyranids. Runtherds tell tales of how the tribe were hunting through the jungles of some remote world when they came across a great fleshy spore encased in glistening amber. Dragging it back to the Ork fleet, they cracked it open and hundreds of clawed, serpentine Tyranids spilled out. The Snakebites hunted the creatures, taking great pleasure in the fact that they seemed to grow rapidly, and no sooner had you bashed one than another one appeared from a vent or drain. Before long the Ork kroozer was infested, and most of the other tribes on board were killed, only the Snakebites surviving in the weird Tyranid jungle their ship had become. By the time the infested kroozer drifted into a system, the Snakebites had finally killed most of the Tyranids on board, having learnt the best ways to crack them open and smash them up. Covered in Tyranid trophies and using alien claws and talons as weapons, they joined up with other Orks, calling themselves the Wyrm-Killa tribe. Having had so much fun hunting the Tyranids in space, the tribe had kept some alive and released them on the first world they came to. While the rest of the Orks bashed the human inhabitants the Wyrm-Killas made sure the Tyranids had time to multiply, so they would make good hunting. By the time the Orks had torn apart the humans they found themselves overrun by Tyranids, and gleefully turned their attentions to this new foe. Since then the Wyrm-Killas have spread Tyranids to dozens of worlds so they can have a good fight wherever they go.

BLOOD AXES

The other clans view the Blood Axes with an uneasy sense of distrust. They trade openly with the Imperium's more isolated worlds, plan their battles in advance, and even consider retreat to be something done on purpose. Qualities that would recommend the Blood Axes as natural leaders amongst most of the galaxy's other races instead see them labelled as treacherous scumbags by the vast majority of greenskins.

In fact, most of the Blood Axes' reputation is undeserved. True, they have made the most contact with the Imperium, occasionally even fighting for the humans as mercenaries, and making extensive use of Imperial war materiel. Then again, every Ork can see the funny side of extorting weapons from human planets only to use them against their former owners.

It doesn't help the Blood Axes' reputation among the tribes that a lot of their young Orks end up in the Stormboyz. These odd Ork formations are a place where a young Ork can rebel against the anarchy of Ork society by following orders, conducting precise military drills and polishing their boots. Heckled and laughed at by most other Orks the Stormboyz spend hours each day marching about and chanting, saluting each other and generally carrying on in very un-Orky ways. The jeers of the other mobs tend to fade away when battle is joined though and the Stormboyz prove their worth. Using potent rokkit packs, they fly into the fray on pillars of smoke and fire. As they age, most Orks leave the Stormboyz for 'proper' mobs, but some gain a taste for it, especially Blood Axes, and will rise to command whole formations of black-booted young Orks.

Blood Axes view the act of getting shot before they reach the enemy lines as a waste of a good fight, and so many have adopted the practice of wearing camouflage. This makes them a target for derision, but in truth the Blood Axes barely notice this. For this reason the clan also has a natural affinity for Kommando mobs, and makes extensive use of them in battle. Unlike other kinds of Orks, Kommandos like to sneak up on their foes, using all the dirty, underhanded tricks they can think of to get the drop on them. Most Orks consider the idea of hiding from a fight or silently creeping through cover a waste of time, if not downright cowardly. What they don't understand is that Kommandos like a good fight just as much as the next Ork, only they know how to get in close without getting shot in the face. There is no greater pleasure for a Kommando than making a good surprise attack, that split second as horror spreads across their victim's face worth all those hours of crawling through the mud.

Blood Axe Warbosses seem to have a better understanding of grand strategy than their compatriots from the other clans, knowing when to combine a Dakkajet strike with a ground attack, or send in a mob of Kommandos. This trait makes them especially dangerous to foes who underestimate the Blood Axes' grasp of actual tactics until it's far too late.

DA BIG RAID

The Blood Axes of Waaagh! Grog tell a story about the greatest Kommando attack ever, known as Da Big Raid. It happened on the world of Vor'sanar, when Waaagh! Grog smashed into the edges of the Tau Empire. Freebooter raids on the Tau planet had been previously repulsed by a huge alien warship with more dakka than anything in the Ork fleet. Called the Korst'la by the Tau and Da Big Dakkaship by the Orks, it stalked the space lanes around Vor'sanar, annihilating anything that trespassed on the Tau Empire. The Korst'la's only weakness was that it needed to use the huge orbital docks around Vor'sanar to refuel and rearm. While Grog knocked the heads of his Freebooter Kaptins together, trying to get a large enough fleet together to storm the Tau planet, a mob of Blood Axe Kommandos came up with a more cunning plan. They would attack the orbital docks while the Korst'la was away, wrecking the Tau station, and denying the warship a place to repair itself or rearm. The Kommandos set out in a looted Tau transport ship, using captured codes to approach the Vor'sanar dockyard under the pretence of having been damaged in an Ork raid and seeking safe harbour. The Tau were initially suspicious of the lone vessel limping into their station, but every demand for identification was met with a satisfactory response, and the idea that Orks could undertake such a ruse was unthinkable to the Tau. It was a horrific surprise then when the vacuum seals opened and Ork Kommandos poured out into the station. By the time the Tau had mustered to repel the invaders, the Kommandos had reached the station's reactors. Smashing them to scrap, they set off a chain reaction, dooming the station and allowing Waaagh! Grog to ransack Vor'sanar and ultimately the entire sector.

DEATHSKULLS

The Deathskulls are plunderers without equal. They are tremendously adept at looting, borrowing, scrounging, scavenging, and stealing things from their fellow Orks, and notoriously bad at giving them back. Given their ingenuity, most Deathskulls would make capable scientists and excellent engineers if their fascination for new things lasted longer than the time it took to steal them.

The Deathskulls see battle as a two-stage process, often hurrying the killing part in an effort to speed along the scavenging spree that follows. After the battle the Boyz really go to work, feverishly stripping the corpses of the fallen of everything from ammunition to bootlaces. Many Deathskulls will take grisly trophies such as their victim's scalp or skull into the bargain. Only when the loot is returned to the camp does the inevitable infighting break out, as the Deathskulls trade, barter and auction off their ill-gotten gains. Other Orks drawn to Deathskulls camps in search of these stolen goods – looking for a specific bit of kit or even something taken from them in the first place – usually leave with less than they came with, as the Deathskulls have the uncanny ability to knock another Ork around the head while going through his pockets at the same time.

Deathskulls do not limit their pillaging to enemy corpses, and anything that can be taken probably will be. Wrecked vehicles are especially popular for this, and the burnt-out hulls of battle tanks, armoured transports or even flyers are all fair game. Dragged off the battlefield, they can either be broken down for bits or taken to a Mek, who will beat some life back into them. More than one foe has been horrified to see one of their own vehicles turned against them, Deathskulls yelling insults from the turrets of their looted vehicle as it rumbles across the battlefield.

The clan uses a horned death's head as its totem, and this symbol is added onto anything its Boyz have stolen to establish ownership over it once and for all. This can also involve painting it blue, which they believe is a lucky colour, and blue handprints and smears on vehicles are also sometimes used as a mark of ownership, regardless of what the current occupants say. The superstitious Deathskulls even use blue warpaint, often going so far as to daub themselves from head to toe in it the night before a battle.

Given the Deathskulls' broad definition of what constitutes personal property, it is little wonder that so many of their clan are Lootas. In fact, most Orks see Deathskulls and Lootas as one and the same – both a bunch of thieving gits one would do well to keep a constant eye on. Lootas are compulsive scavengers who also have a weakness for large guns. They seek out the biggest and best weapons they can carry, often getting Meks to cobble them together into even bigger guns, so heavy that they have to balance them on their meaty shoulders. These 'deffguns', as they are dubbed, are among the deadliest weapons an Ork can wield, and in battle they make a tremendous racket as they tear apart the enemy with bullets, blasts and bolts.

GORK'S OTHER FOOT

Nabrot Stub-fingers is renowned among the Deathskulls of Octarius for his kleptomania. The saying goes that if Nabrot can't loot it, it ain't worth stealing. This is something the Ork has proved time and again, making off with piles of teef, shiny weapons and poorly guarded vehicles. Nabrot's mob goes into battle with many of the larger things he has nicked, such as battle tanks and big guns, all festooned with the mob's glyphs and painted in his favoured colours. Other stuff he pinches just because it amuses him on some level, like the statue of the Emperor from the spire of the Illuminous Cathedral on Tobin's Rest. The Sisters of Battle defending the shrine world vowed unending vengeance against the invaders after Nabrot drove into battle with the crudely defaced statue lashed upside down to the front of his wagon. The most impressive thing Nabrot ever looted was the Baneblade super-heavy tank known as Gork's Other Foot. When the Overfiend of Octarius turned his blood-red eyes on the forge world of Kernak III, Nabrot and his Deathskulls followed the Warboss into battle. The Cadian defenders reeled before the Ork assault, their lines holding only thanks to the guns of several Baneblades. Nabrot immediately decided he had to have one for himself. Leading a small force of Deathskulls, Nabrot found a way through the vast sewer complex of Kernak and into its heavily defended factorums. Whilst his Boyz caused a destructive distraction, Nabrot stole a Baneblade and blasted his way back to the Ork lines. He dubbed the tank Gork's Foot, saying it was so it could give the enemy a good kicking. This lasted until it was pointed out by another Ork that the Overfiend's Gargant was called Gork's Foot, to which Nabrot replied, 'Well then, this is his other foot.'

FREEBOOTERZ

Ork Freebooterz are notorious pirates and thieves, plying the void in smoking, sparking ships with the intent of causing as much mayhem and destruction as possible. They prey upon anyone foolish enough to stray into their hunting grounds, screaming out of the dark on plumes of fire to blast apart their foes. When an enemy vessel is crippled or foolishly tries to surrender, the Freebooterz will smash their way on board, killing anything that moves and stealing anything that doesn't. The Freebooterz will then haul their booty back to their hidden bases and count their ill-gotten gains.

When a Warboss wants to invade a planet, he calls on fleets of Freebooterz to see off enemy ships and clear the way for the Orks to get down to the surface. For this service Freebooterz claim exorbitant scavenging rights as well as a fortune in teef, and a Warboss has little choice but to pay up if he wants their help, as Freebooterz that don't get their price often simply vanish into the void in search of more loot. Even if a Freebooter's terms are met, he might still get distracted by better prospects, the lure of easy plunder enough to sway most kaptins. Whether they fight alongside a Waaagh! or tear around the void raiding planets and stealing ships, Freebooterz often become disgustingly rich, leading many to become Flash Gitz.

Ork Freebooterz are by no means always Flash Gitz, but all Flash Gitz eventually end up as Freebooterz. Arrogant and boorish, a Nob who fancies himself a Flash Git will normally alienate himself in short order from the rest of his tribe. Whether because of his grating self-aggrandisement, eating the local Big Mek's favourite grot oiler without permission, or committing the cardinal sin of strutting about with a bigger, shinier shoota than the Warboss, a Flash Git will normally find himself ejected from his tribe. When a whole band of Nobz get ideas above their place in the order of things within the tribe all at once, it can lead to bloody infighting. This will usually end up with the departure – at gunpoint or otherwise – of a whole mob of newly freebootin' Flash Gitz.

However they find their way into this new situation, Flash Git mobs will quickly take to the Freebooter life. Fighting as mercenaries allows successful Gitz to accumulate vast sums of wealth in a short space of time. Even better, they can gleefully spend it all on themselves without a Warboss around to take his cut. With teef galore flowing into their coffers, successful mobs of Flash Gitz will soon be riding through the void in their very own kill kroozer while wielding the kind of firearms that Deathskulls Lootas can only dream of stealing. They bedeck themselves with natty finery, even their grot minions get stuffed into gold-buttoned frock coats and brag loudly of their masters' wealth. Flash Gitz also sport profusions of piercings, furs, glyph-plates, brightly coloured pirate garb and extravagant hats. All of this showy nonsense does absolutely nothing though to hide the hulking, muscular bulk and bestial lethality of the Flash Gitz themselves.

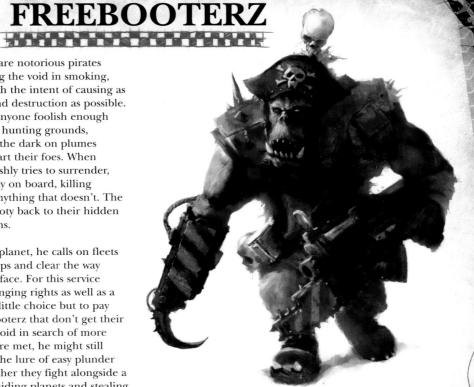

KAPTIN BADRUKK

Kaptin Badrukk is the greatest Freebooter of his age, a monstrous, roaring privateer bedecked in barbarous finery. Badrukk's Flash Gitz carry enough firepower into battle to level a well-defended hab-block, and the Kaptin totes the most fearsome firearm of the lot. Badrukk and his villainous crew are legends among their own cutthroat subculture, thundering through space in their oversized Kill Kroozer Da Blacktoof, and they have fought at the side of every major Warboss worth following in recent history. Wherever the Kaptin and his ladz make planetfall, misery and destruction are sure to follow, for Badrukk's Flash Gitz are superlative reavers who live to commit murder and cause mayhem, stealing everything they can get their claws on. Years ago, Badrukk was chased out of the Bad Moons clan on charges of having too many teef for his own good. From the day of his exile, Badrukk's accomplishments have far outstripped those of his fellow Freebooter kaptins. Fighting alongside the fleet of Warlord Garaghak, Badrukk blunted a tendril of the Tyranid Hive Fleet Kraken with an all-guns-blazing raid upon the Norn Queen at its heart. During the War of Dakka, his warriors outshot a Tau Hunter cadre. Some even claim that the Kaptin personally brought down a Freeblade Knight armed with nought but a hair squig and several inebriated Snotlings, though it seems likely that such tales have grown in the telling. Most recently, Badrukk has been engaged in a series of bloody skirmishes against Space Wolves forces deep in the Sanctus Reach. A rumour persists that these raids are being performed at the behest of a shady and extremely generous employer, but Badrukk is playing his cards extremely close to his chest.

GATHERING THE WAAAGH!

An Ork Waaagh! is war on an apocalyptic scale. Orks beyond counting swarm from one world to the next. Whole civilisations are exterminated and defenders' armies laid to waste as the Orks plough ever onward in an unstoppable tide.

Orks need battle just as humans need food and drink. Due to their warlike nature, they constantly fight amongst themselves, or launch piratical raids upon nearby enemies. Such conflicts tend to be small-scale or localised. They never really develop beyond random outbursts of violence and looting. However, Ork populations can reach a critical mass that leads to a full-scale planetary migration. This is known as a Waaagh!, a crusade of pure aggression that crashes through star systems in an orgy of violence.

A Waaagh! usually starts small, even as small as a single Ork visited by dreams of carnage. He will hammer his dreams of conquest into his subordinates, and then lead them in attacks against other Ork warbands. With each victory, the new Warboss' legend grows, and more followers flock to his blood-soaked banner. As he fights to retain command of his ever-growing horde against a constant stream of challengers, he will subsume the armies of those he conquers into his own tribe, and as news of his prowess spreads ever further, the trickle of reinforcements becomes a green flood.

Drawn in by the Warboss' reputation, Ork Meks will start to collaborate on more and more outlandish projects as the Waaagh! grows, building even larger war machines and guns. Smoke belching mobile fortresses and titanic engines of battle are cobbled together out of nothing more than scrap metal and heavy-handed enthusiasm. Gorkanauts and Morkanauts appear in growing numbers, their pilots seeking out the Waaagh! with a feverish intensity. Whole mobs of Mekboyz raise towering scaffolds within which Stompas and even Gargants start to take shape, these mighty effigies igniting some primitive drive within the minds of the Orks who see them, causing the flow of Waaagh! energy they subconciously generate to reach fever pitch.

At this stage there is still much rivalry between the various clans and tribes, and each will strive to outdo all the others in terms of the sheer destruction that can be wrought by its war machines. Those Meks without the resources to construct Stompas and Gargants will instead create mobs of clanking Killa Kans and Deff Dreads, or Battlewagons from which the Warbosses can lead their armies to war.

Soon the emergent Waaagh! begins to span worlds instead of just continents. Entire native populations are forced into slavery merely to manufacture ammunition for the horde's guns. Crude factory-ships and war hulks are bashed into shape, the better to transport the Ork armies into battle.

When the lure of imminent bloodshed can be resisted no more, the deadly fervour washing through the horde overflows. Teeming Ork armies mass and swell with a roar like savage oceans, and the skies fill with crude and bulky Ork space-faring vessels.

The grand musters that precede a full-scale Ork invasion are an awe-inspiring sight. As the Orks gather for battle, smoke from thousands of oily engines fills the sky. The ground trembles beneath great wheels, tracks and the thunderous strides of towering Gargants. Armies of greenskins stretch across the horizon, raising their banners high to proclaim their reputations and allegiances, their warcries audible for miles around. Looming Gorkanauts and Morkanauts, bizarre artillery pieces and force field generators chug, clank and buzz amidst the green throng. Armadas of rusty vehicles raise roiling thunderheads of dust into the atmosphere, whilst Dakkajets roar overhead leaving contrails of filthy smoke. Speed Freeks rev their engines, and the Boyz fire their guns into the air as a carpet of Gretchin spreads out in front of the army.

Eventually, the battlefield is barely visible beneath the endless sea of green, each Ork warrior certain that the ground will soon be stained red. Here the power of the Waaagh! is palpable as a wave of raw aggression, and the Orks believe Gork and Mork are gazing eagerly down from the Warp to see how their warriors will fare.

Then as one, with an almighty bellow, the Orks surge forwards, and another world is plunged into unending war.

THE GREAT WAAAGH!

It is generally thought within the Imperium that over the last century or so, the Orks have become even more aggressive and warlike than ever before, and the numbers of Waaaghs! being recorded in all five Segmentums is increasing.

The Imperium has long theorised that the greenskin race possesses low-level background psychic abilities, a kind of gestalt Warp resonance. Orks, of course, neither know nor care about such things. Yet as Warp space becomes more turbulent, so the Orks too are becoming ever more belligerent. This rise in new Waaaghs! has been most notable around Warp space anomalies and regions plagued by Warp storms, with hundreds of greenskin invasion forces emerging from these areas every year.

Members of the Ordo Xenos have noticed a trend in the translations of glyph-sequences found in Ork camps, which speak increasingly of 'da call of da gods'. a phenomenon felt most keenly by the nomadic Gorkanaut and Morkanaut pilots. The emergence of Weirdboyz seems to be increasing exponentially also, with many claiming that they see visions sent by Gork and Mork. On thousands of worlds the ominous silhouettes of Gargants rise against the war-torn skies. The Orks' foes can only watch in horrified bewilderment as the phenomenon known as the Great Waaagh! sees the greenskins flooding across the galaxy in numbers never before witnessed, slaughtering everything in their path as they go.

WAAAGH! GRUKK

The Butcher of Obstiria, the Bane of Eyrok and the Scourge of the Sanctus Reach – these are all names earned by Warboss Grukk Face-rippa for his bloody deeds. Rumoured to be blessed by Gork himself, Grukk has never lost a battle, the brutish Warboss smashing his way from one world to the next, always looking for the next big scrap.

THE TWO TRIBES

Once an Ork Boy in the Skullcracker Goff tribe of Krugg the Tyrant on the desert world of Eyrok, Grukk fought for Krugg's tribe for many years against the Split-Grin Bad Moons, with little thought beyond his next fight. Eyrok had once been an Imperial planet, and the two tribes spent much of their time at war amongst its ruins, their Trukks and bikes tearing across the scorching dunes and through the skeletal remains of the hive cities. Even then Grukk was bigger and stronger than the other Orks, and Krugg kept a wary eye on him ready to put him back into place if he stepped out of line. The only thing that stopped Krugg throwing Grukk down the biggest sinkhole he could find was that the Ork was just too handy in a fight. Fate then took a hand in Grukk's life when it sent the Big Mek Mogrok to Eyrok. The Mek had been marooned there by a tribe of Freebooterz, who had decided that firing the Mek at a planet was easier than paying him for the work he did to their ship, and was now trying to build his own ship from scrap. When Grukk came upon the Mek he was going to give him a good kicking, until Mogrok changed his mind.

WARBOSS GRUKK

Mogrok convinced Grukk that rather than fighting a few Orks on some backwater planet, he could be conquering whole star systems. It took a while, but the Mek eventually awoke a spark of ambition in Grukk. The Ork charged back to the Goff fort and smashed his way into Krugg's ramshackle hut, knocking the Warboss from his feet with a roar of challenge. The Tyrant fought back with savage brutality, battering Grukk bloody. The two Orks tore the fort apart in their struggle, and eventually Krugg caught Grukk with a thunderous backhand blow of his saw-fisted power klaw, hurling his brutish challenger through a mudbrick wall into the dusty courtyard beyond. As he loomed over Grukk's crumpled form, Krugg prepared to land the finishing blow. Grukk's will to kill drove him to his feet at the last moment, grabbing the Tyrant's roaring saw-klaw and forcing it inexorably backward. Green sinews shook and muscles bulged as the two Orks strained against each other, yet Grukk was stronger. Krugg's eyes widened in horror just before his arm broke with a rotten crack, and the klaw's roaring saw-blade chewed hungrily into his face. Blood flew in sheets, and with that Warboss Grukk Face-rippa was born.

Within a week, Warboss Grukk had united the Orks of Eyrok, crushing any rivals to his position. As he stood over the fallen Warlord of the Split-grin tribe, Mogrok was there again, talking in Grukk's ear, telling him about some nearby worlds where there was fighting to be had. Now with free access to all the scrap he could use, the Big Mek hammered a ship together and found the Freebooterz that had marooned him on Eyrok. He brought Grukk with him to teach them a lesson, and those that survived the ensuing battle soon joined up with the Warboss.

Eyrok was on the edge of the Sanctus Sub-sector, and was considered a dead world be the Imperium. It was therefore a surprise for Sector Lord Vargan when a tide of Orks swept across his outlying systems. What began as isolated reports and garbled astropathic missives quickly built into an avalanche of desperate cries for aid. Grukk mercilessly ravaged the toxic jungle moons of Palos, breaking the great crystal dome of its blessed city and flooding it with poisons while his warriors looted and killed. On the penal outpost of Night's End, the Orks turned the prison into a giant fighting pit, throwing in squigs, grots and Boyz while placing bets on how long the prisoners would last against them. When Sector Lord Vargan sent his periphery fleet against Grukk, the Orks attacked them in the midst of an asteroid field. Ork and Imperial vessels were hammered with rocks as they as blasted each other to scrap, the Orks ramming, battering and boarding dozens of Imperial vessels. With every raid and battle more Orks flocked to Grukk's banner, and his legend took root in the minds of greenskins across the breadth of the Sanctus Sub-sector. In the space of a few short years, a sector of space considered desolate was teeming with Orks, all bawling the name Grukk into the dark.

THE RED WAAAGH!

By the time Grukk reached the Sanctus Reach he had billions of Orks following in his wake. Only a few little obstacles stood in the Orks' way, most notably the Space Marine world of Obstiria, home to the Obsidian Glaives Chapter. Five companies of the Chapter defended their planet, led by their Chapter Master Midnias, a scarred veteran of countless wars against the greenskins. Despite Grukk's numbers, Midnias has assured the Sector Lord that he could halt the Ork incursion before it plunged even deeper into the sub-sector.

Even before Grukk reached Obstiria, Freebooterz and mobs of Evil Sunz were racing ahead to be the first ones to attack the Space Marines. Kaptin Dakbad Flamegut was the first to descend upon the planet, his kill kroozers charging at the Obsidian Glaives' orbital defences. Hundreds of thousands of Orks reached the surface of Obstiria through a hail of anti-aircraft fire, and laid siege to the Penumbral Spike, fortress monastery of the Obsidian Glaives. The Spike was an impressive fortification, rising hundreds of metres above the radiation-washed plains of Obstiria's polar continent, its spire permanently cloaked in thick cloud. In the three millennia since the creation of the Chapter, it had never fallen to a foe. Soon Orks scaled the fortress walls, bellowing war cries while the Space Marines blasted at them from above. Numerous times the Orks bludgeoned or shot their way into the fortress, Midnias personally leading counter-attacks to throw them back, and for seven days and nights the Obsidian Glaives held back the Orks, the loss of each

fallen Space Marine keenly felt, each section of their fortress defiled a stain upon their honour. Finally, on the dawn of the eighth day, the tide of Orks seemed to slacken, leaving the Space Marines to count their dead. Then Grukk arrived.

The Orks that had attacked Obstiria so far had been but the merest tip of the Red Waaagh!, a grim taste of things to come. When Midnias learned of the Warlord's coming he knew his only hope was to slay Grukk. The Battle of Black Gulch was Midnias' final attempt to kill the Warboss. At first the Space Marines caught the Orks by surprise, slaying thousands as they fell upon the horde, but then the Orks' numbers started to come to bear. Into their midst Midnias soared, roaring across the battlefield on his jump pack to engage Grukk, his blade moving in a blurr to hack off the Ork's head. Grukk turned at the last moment, taking the blow on his thickly muscled shoulder, roaring in pain. As Midnias raised his blade for another strike, Grukk lashed out and wrapped a meaty fist around the blade. The Chapter Master strained with his considerable strength against the Ork to free his sword, but Grukk pivotied against the Space Marine's weight and delivered a thunderous uppercut that tore Midnias' helm, head and all, clean from his shoulders. Thus ended the Obsidian Glaives. Their commander dead, the Space Marines valiantly attempted to defend their world for a further three days, fighting a battle they could not hope to win against the overwhelming numbers of Grukk's hordes. With Obstiria crushed and the Sanctus Reach aflame, only Alaric Prime remained defiant, and the Red Waaagh! gathered once more for war.

GRUKK'S RAMPAGE

SANCTUS
Stellar Primo Nova

TERENDIL
Paradise World
DECLARED PERDITAS
773.M32

THE WRATH OF GORK

SQUIRE'S REST
Agri World

MALAGHAI MORCA
Rogue Trading Post

OBSTIRIA
Home World of the Obsidian Glaives

GHUL JENSEN
Hive World

ALARIC PRIME
Knight World

WARBANDS OF WAAAGH! GRUKK

As Grukk's legend grew, many tribes of Orks flocked to his banner, eager to fight in the great battles that this new Warlord would lead them into. What began as two tribes on Eyrok and a few thousand Boyz would grow into a sector-spanning Waaagh! of billions of Orks, capable of bringing ruin and death to whole worlds.

ORK TRIBES OF EYROK

Once he'd gotten a taste for power, Grukk brought all the tribes of Eyrok to heel in a single bloody week. By the time he was ready to strike out into the stars he had a sizable force under his control, and those few remainging greenskins foolish enough to stand in his way were crushed under the lumbering footsteps of his followers.

BIG MEK MOGROK

Always close at hand, Mogrok made sure Grukk was attacking the best worlds and keeping the tribes in line. Filled with all kinds of technological inspiration, Mogrok always seems to have another trick in his bag of scrap, often pulling something out at the last minute to turn the tide in favour of Grukk and his boyz. When, during the Battle of Bonewash, Grukk's Skullcrackers were ambushed by rebel grots of the Red-toe Tribe it was Mogrok's shokk-traktor truck that sucked up the diminutive warriors and sprayed them across the desert like green and red confetti.

SKULLCRACKER BOYZ

Emulating the mindless rage of Grukk, the Skullcracker Goff Boyz became meaner than ever. Wherever the hulking Warboss charged into the fray dozens of his Boyz were always close at hand, their bunched green muscles and cruel beady eyes reflecting the rage and violence of their leader. Over time, the biggest and strongest of the Skullcrackers formed a personal bodyguard for Grukk, these Skull-Nobz covered in scars and trophies from their many victories.

KAPTIN DAKBAD'S FLASHGITZ

The firepower of the Flash Gitz was once the bane of the Skullcrackers, until Grukk turned them against his enemies instead. Kaptin Dakbad in particular knew a good thing when it came up and punched him in the face, siding with Grukk and riding the wave of carnage and loot all the way to the Sanctus Reach. It also helped Dakbad's position with Grukk that the Warboss needed his ships if he was ever to get off Eyrok.

WASTELAND WARBIKES

Many of the Orks of Eyrok roared to war on mechanised chargers built from the rusting remains of the hive cities on that long deserted human world, and the revving engines of thousands of bikes heralding the tribe's arrival.

SCRAP-TRUKKS

With such an abundance of scrap metal on Eyrok, the Meks not only built bikes and Battlewagons for their bosses, but also Trukks by the score for themselves so that they could tow it back to their workshops. Most of the wars on Eyrok before the rise of Grukk were over scrap, Orks from every tribe both fighting for and fighting with bits of twisted metal or parts of engine. More than one Ork was bludgeoned to death by a tyre or impaled on a rusty set of bike forks during those turbulent times.

GRUKK'S SANCTUS RAIDERS

Once free of Eyrok, Grukk raided worlds all along the edges of the Sanctus Sub-sector, all the while gathering more Orks to join in with his unchecked rampage. Drawn by the promise of piles of teef and war on an unimaginable scale, thousands of Freebooterz joined Grukk, their vessels allowing him to strike when and where he wanted.

KAPTIN DAKBAD FIREGUT

The first Freebooter to fall in with Grukk, Dakbad and his pirates formed the vanguard of the Ork raiders. Dakbad's ships had spent years raiding the worlds surrounding Eyrok with the reckless violence typical of any Freebooter worth his bloodthirsty reputation. When Grukk offered the kaptin a chance to share in the riches of battle, Dakbad didn't take long to convince. Those worlds that had once been too well defended or too strong for the Freebooterz fleet to attack alone would now fall under the meaty fist of Grukk.

GASHRAKK DA FLASH

Drawn to Grukk's Waaagh! by riches untold, Gashrakk took over as Warboss of the Split-Grin tribe. Ripe for some rough leadership after Grukk staved in the skull of their last boss, the Split-Grin tribe quickly fell into line behind Gashrakk. In the time-honoured tradition of the Bad Moons clan, to gain leadership of the Split-Grins he bribed most of its Nobz with the best guns and choppas teef could buy. Those who did not fall into line soon found themselves the targets of their former comrades' new arsenal.

SKULLCRACKER MEGANOBZ

Assaulting planets and boarding ships requires huge armoured Orks, and the biggest, most armoured Orks following Grukk were his Skullcracker Meganobz. Only the toughest of the Skull-Nobz earned a place within the Meganobz. Those who were first to get a suit of mega armour, however, had to not only be strong enough to wear it but mean enough to keep it too.

SPLIT-GRIN DAKKAJETS

With all his teef and connections, Gashrakk got together a squadron of Dakkajets, their screaming engines filling the skies above the worlds Grukk attacked. Notorious show-offs, the Split-Grin Dakkajets would spend almost as much time barrel-rolling and diving down from the sky as going where Grukk told them. Even so, as soon as any enemy fighters appeared the Dakkajets would fall on them like locusts, their hammering guns and howling jets filling the sky.

THE RED WAAAGH!

When Grukk reached the Sanctus Reach it was at the head of a bellowing, chanting sea of greenskins – amongst them millions of Orks driven into a mad frenzy at the prospect of battle on a scale few of them had been part of before. Unwittingly (or perhaps intentionally on Mogrok's part) Grukk now commanded a mighty Waaagh!.

BADDFRAG'S LOOTED WAGONS

The Warboss Baddfrag led many of Grukk's armoured and shooty wagons, lots of them pinched from the humies but made even more killy. Often the first things to hit the ground when Grukk invaded a planet, Baddfrag's looted wagons would rumble forward, smashing anything in their path in a rising tide of rusting metal and flame-belching barrels. On Phenos IX, Baddfrag led the charge across the ancient energy bridge connecting the hive primus to the world's jungle-choked mainland. Ramming through the Imperium's defences, Baddfrag sent scores of enemy tanks tumbling off the bridge and into the boiling seas hundreds of metres below. In the aftermath of the battle, Baddfrag used mobs of grots tethered to cables to fish out the wrecks so he could press them into service again.

WINGNUTZ'S FLYBOYZ

Wingnutz was skyboss of the Flyboyz, a huge formation of Dakkajets, Burna-bommer and Blitza-bommers which would darken the skies in the vanguard of the Red Waaagh!. So eager was Wingnutz to get into combat that his Boyz would lash their planes to the outside of scrap ships, cutting them free as they fell through a planet's atmosphere. The Flyboyz would then plague the skies of the world, shooting down anything in their sights and dropping bombs on targets below. Wingnutz himself became notorious for his death-defying strafing runs over battlefields, his Dakkajet passing only a few metres above the heads of startled Orks and their terrified enemies alike.

BOGROT BONES' GARGANTUAN SQUIGGOTH

There were huge numbers of Snakebites in the Red Waaagh!, but none meaner than Bogrot Bones and his pet Gargantuan Squiggoth, Stompy. In battle, Stompy lived up to its name, trampling entire companies into the ground under its bulk, often oblivious to the mayhem it was causing. The small-brained beast could only concentrate on one thing at a time, however, and was easily confused. Bogrot Bones would yell and bawl, trying to goad it into going where he wanted, though Stompy, often seeing something shiny, would thunder off in a random direction. This happened on numerous occasions during the Red Waaagh!, the huge monster either turning the tide of battle inadvertently or causing carnage among the Ork hordes as it crashed through its own allies. One example of this occurred on Sybel III; Stompy broke open the fortress when he spied the shiny medals on the chest of the fort's Imperial Guard commander. The officer was waving and yelling to his men from the top of the wall, unaware he was leading the Squiggoth on. Stompy headbutted its way through the wall and gave chase to the terrified commander as he ran up the seven tiers of the fortress, trying to close gates behind him and ordering men to cover his flight. In the end, Stompy cornered and pulverised the officer in the heart of the citadel as thousands of Orks poured in through the breaches he had left behind.

WEIRDBOYZ AND BIG REDD DA WARPHEAD

Though none of the other Orks liked them, the Weirdboyz, like Big Redd, did their bit for the Waaagh!, blowing up heads with their raw psychic power. In battle, the Weirdboyz would vomit forth raw Warp-energies, overcome with the might of the Waaagh!. This could have all manner of unforeseen consequences as their psychic powers ran amok; heads would burst like over-ripe fruit, limbs would snap like twigs and organs rupture as pulsing shockwaves of power rolled out from the Weirdboyz. Big Redd was the worst of them, and other Orks didn't like to hang around the odd-looking Weirdboy, even when he wasn't thrashing about and babbling like a brain-damaged grot. Strange things followed Big Redd around like a lingering stench, mumbling and gnashing. Big Redd himself didn't seem to mind, as he was always muttering under his breath and talking to things only he could see anyway.

GOFFBOSS DROGG

Grukk had lots and lots of Goffs in his Waaagh!, and Goffboss Drogg was charged with keeping them in line so the Warboss could concentrate on just smashing stuff; Goffs have a habit of getting carried away when there's a scrap in the offing. Most of the time, Grukk didn't mind if the boyz didn't do what they were told, as long as they were knocking heads together. Those other times, he made sure Drogg was nearby to restore order. On the planet of Absedia, Grukk used his Goff hordes to break the back of the Ministorum's defences. Drogg made sure the boyz focussed on Absedia's Abbey of the Ardent Dawn, rounding up mobs distracted by burning up the planet's peaceful countryside and sending them up the mountain toward the humie fortress. It was also Drogg's cunning tactic to use the big statues surrounding the abbey to smash down its walls, toppling them over to the deafening cheers of the gathering Ork horde.

MOGROK'S BIG GUNZ

The Big Mek supplied Grukk with a massive arsenal of artillery of all types, enough to line them up for miles, wheel-to-wheel and lay down massive, if unpredictable, barrages. At the outset of the battle for the Sanctus Reach, Mogrok filled the hulls of Grukk's Freebooter armada full of guns of all shapes and sizes, looted from dead enemies or hammered together out of scrap. Often, there was no way of knowing just what would come out of a gun's barrel until it was fired. However, there was one problem. The grots manning the guns did not have a clue how to fire them. Constantly looking over their shoulder to see if they were about to get a slap from the runt herder, the grots would often spend the first few minutes of the battle prodding and grappling with the guns, trying to figure out how they worked. Nevertheless, the outcome was always devastating – either for the enemy or the grots.

DA FISTS OF GORK

Grukk's prized Gorkanauts had a fearsome and well-deserved reputation for carnage. These towering engines of death were always at the forefront of any battle, their claws and guns ripping into the foe. Inside their well armoured hulls the grinning Nobz would try to out-do each other, killing enemies in successively more spectacular ways or racing against each other to be the first to get into the fray. By the end of the war, each Gorkanaut had amassed an impressive tally of kills.

SPLIT-GRIN BAD MOONS

All Bad Moons Orks have a well-deserved reputation for being as proud of their loot as of their prowess in battle. The Split-Grin tribe are among the worst of their kind, and have amassed piles of teef in recent years. Following the trail of destruction sown by Grukk and the Red Waaagh!, Gashrakk da Flash and his Split-Grins rival Grukk's own tribe in size and status.

A FIST FULL OF TEEF

For years the Split-Grin Bad Moons scraped out an existence on Eyrok skirmishing with their rivals the Skullcrackers. Their Warboss, Skagfing, was content to lead his Boyz in the brawl with the Goffs and make some teef in the process, trading with Freebooterz for shiny stuff. The big guns of the clan kept the Skullcrackers in check, and Skagfing liked to make jokes about poor old Krugg the 'Tyrant' who couldn't afford a good shoota. The Split-Grin tribe might not have been huge, but they had the best loot, and the biggest guns to keep other Orks from getting their hands on it.

This all changed when Grukk met Mogrok and decided to take control of all Eyrok's Orks. Skagfing had only recently heard about his rival's death when Grukk and his lads smashed their way into the Bad Moons camp, the Goff Warlord sacrificing loads of Boyz as he charged to in pin Skagfing down, stand on his chest, and messily rip his face from his skull. In a single bloody blow, the Split-Grins were absorbed into the Skullcrackers and Grukk took control of the tribe. In Skagfing's place a bunch of Nobs tried to bully their way to the top, but none of them could match the raw aggression and prodigious size of Grukk.

Fragmented and leaderless, the Split-Grin tribe became inferior to the Skullcrackers. Grukk used the tribe for its massive guns and kustom weapons, draining their stockpiles to build up his warband. The Split-Grin tribe also gave Grukk access to the Sanctus Sub-sector's Freebooterz, giving the Ork Warboss a way off Eyrok and out into the void. Of course, Freebooterz' tastes are just as extravagant as Bad Moons, and so as soon as Grukk's warband took to the stars, the fortunes of the Split-Grins changed again.

DA FLASHY FREEBOOTER

Gashrakk da Flash was once first mate to none other than Kaptin Badrukk, the famous Ork pirate. According to rumour, even Badrukk had gotten sick of Gashrakk's swaggering pretension and so had forced him off his ship. Heading off on his own, Gashrakk had massed a small fleet of kroozers and was haunting the Sanctus Sub-sector when Grukk left Eyrok. Seeing an opportunity to increase his wealth, and to have a good fight too, Gashrakk 'happened' to cross paths with the Goff Warboss and offered his services. It was completely by chance that the Freebooter fell in with the Split-Grin Bad Moons, but as soon as he did the Orks knew they had met a leader they could profit under.

Gashrakk was something of an anomaly among Orks; he was always clean, his kit polished to a high shine and his colourful armour and clothes bright and unstained. In fact, Gashrakk's obsession with his wargear extended beyond his personal appearance and to his ships and weapons, each one buffed to a dull shine. Gashrakk would use mobs of grots to keep his gear in pristine condition, and as soon as his armour took a scratch or his boots lost their lustre a grot would be there to polish them up or, failing that, to hurry along with a replacement. The Freebooter boasted that he had never used the same gun more than once – such was his wealth that he would throw his shoota away after each fusillade, a grot gun-caddy rushing forward to offer up a fresh one.

This mixture of arrogance and vanity were just what the Split-Grins wanted, and its Nobz and Boyz fell into line behind Gashrakk, dubbing him 'da Flash'. He, in turn, made sure that no one could mistake the Split-Grin Bad Moons for any other mob of Orks, and that when they turned up there could be no doubt they were the richest warband around. The Freebooter surrounded his tribe with Meks, keeping them plied with teef and scrap so he always had the best kustom wargear. Gashrakk spread these choice items amongst his favoured Boyz, ensuring the Split-Grins always had the best weapons, wagons and armour, and the other tribes were only able to look on in envy.

At this point, the Freebooter had the first sparks of an idea about how he might become the richest Warboss ever. By following Grukk's Waaagh! into the biggest battles and relying on the Split-Grins' fearsome firepower, he could keep his tribe's losses low, ensuring that any loot ended up finding its way into the holds of his ships.

KILL THINGS, TAKE STUFF

Not long after Grukk started raiding the edges of the Sanctus Sub-sector, Gashrakk figured out that as long as he avoided the big Warboss' temper (no small feat) he could talk the single-minded Goff into giving his Split-Grin tribe the choicest enemies to fight and the best bits of a world to attack. On the moons of Palos, while Grukk's mobs cracked their way into the domed cities, Gashrakk plundered the world's diamond mines, allowing the tribe's Meks to use the gems as lenses in kustom blastaz or big gunz, and the Painboyz to give the richest Nobz new sets of 'shiny teef'. On the prison planet of Night's End, the Split-Grin tribe made piles of teef running the pit fights, Gashrakk personally blasting one particularly tough prisoner to bits when it looked like he might upset the odds.

More than once Gashrakk put Grukk's loot in his own ships 'for safe-keeping' and waited for the Warboss' attention to be drawn to another fight instead. Mogrok would have challenged Gashrakk for trying to use the Red Waaagh! for his own ends, if the Big Mek wasn't doing precisely the same thing himself. In fact, the effectiveness of the Split-Grin tribe's kustom weaponry allowed Gashrakk to get Mogrok and his Mek followers to make several Gorkanauts and Morkanauts for the Split-Grins. The Freebooter even managed to lay claim to one of Mogrok's Stompas, and the Split-Grins were soon accompanied in battle by an ever-expanding horde of smoke-belching walkers.

GASHRAKK'S BAD MOONS

The Split-Grin Bad Moons are about the best-equipped Orks around, and deadly in a fight too – just ask their Warboss, the legendary Gashrakk da Flash.

WARBOSS GASHRAKK DA FLASH

Gashrakk is the Warboss of the Split-Grin Bad Moons, the richest Ork of the wealthiest tribe in the Sanctus Sub-sector. Years of looting worlds in the wake of Waaagh! Grukk have filled Gashrakk's holds with all manner of weapons and equipment; the Freebooter turned Warboss has turned around the fortunes of the Split-Grin Bad Moon Tribe.

PAINBOY KUTRAG

Gashrakk is the only Ork who can afford Kutrag's ridiculous rates, keeping the Painboy supplied with teef so he will fix up the Split-Grin Boyz. Often, 'fixing' an Ork means making him better in some new and unusual way; Kutrag has a reputation for hacking off perfectly good limbs so he can replace them with something better.

GASHRAKK'S FLASH GITZ

Not only do Gashrakk's Flash Gitz have the biggest, most shooty guns but they also have the shiniest. Gashrakk makes sure that his boyz got the best stuff from Grukk's loot, and the Warboss is often oblivious to the Freebooter's skimming off the top. This treasured plunder often takes the form of guns, or parts to make bigger guns, and the Split-Grin Boyz spend piles of teef on Meks to make them even more shooty.

BROKE TEEF LOOTAS

Even in the Split-Grin tribe there are some Orks considered poor, with broken, stumpy teef. These Boyz have to steal things to get rich and so make the best Lootas. They are also often amongst the first Orks to get to the foe's battle line, not because they are the bravest but because they want to make sure they get the first chance to go through the spoils left in the wake of the fight.

FLASHY SKYBOYZ

Gashrakk likes Stormboyz because, like him, they prefer to keep themselves clean and polish their kit all the time. However, he has never got used to the way they insist on saluting him when he walks past.

DEFFKRUNCHER

A Split-Grin Gorkanaut, Deffkruncher is a proper example of an Orky killing machine. The lumbering walker is always a welcome sight for Gashrakk's tribe, its conspicuous yellow hull towering over the fray while its aresenal of guns spits death in all directions.

FORTSMASHA

The Stompa Fortsmasha is Gashrakk's pride and joy, and the Warboss is sure to be near it on the battlefield so he can glory in the destruction it wreaks. Between fights, the Split-Grin tribe are always trying to make it look more garish, adding gaudy Bad Moons colours so that enemies cannot miss the effigy before it brings about their deaths.

WAAAGH! GHAZGHKULL

BLESSED BY GORK

Ghazghkull began his life as a common Goff trooper on the backwater planet of Urk. During a raid upon a Space Marine command sanctum, Ghazghkull was shot in the face by a bolter shell. It pulped a large area of his cranium and caused extensive brain damage. Had he died then, history might have been very different but a Deathskulls Painboy called Mad Dok Grotsnik was close at hand, and replaced part of Ghazghkull's cerebrum with bioniks made from adamantium. It may be that these bioniks triggered some latent psychic power or it may be that Ghazghkull simply suffers from delusions, but for whatever reason, from that point on Ghazghkull claimed to be in direct contact with the Ork gods of war Gork and Mork.

Some mysterious power certainly favours Ghazghkull, for his rise to power among the tribes of Urk was meteoric, and he soon fought his way through the ranks until he achieved the position of supreme planetary warlord. Orks respect strength, courage and battle prowess, and it could not be denied that Ghazghkull possessed all of these qualities in abundance. In addition, he had something that most Warbosses lack: vision. He stirred the Orks of Urk with impassioned speeches, telling them how it was their mission to conquer the galaxy. Wherever Ghazghkull went, he united warring tribes with an overwhelming sense of destiny.

Over the course of the following six years, Ghazghkull brutally conquered the remaining tribes of Urk. He clobbered Warlord Dregmek of the Deathskulls, outwitted Warboss Snazzdakka of the Bad Moons, and out-raced Grand Speedboss Shazfrag of the Evil Sunz. During an incredibly bloody week he subdued the vast hordes of Snakebite Warboss Grudbolg, decapitating the scarred old monster twice before finally winning his loyalty. Ghazghkull's empire now spanned a world, but this was only the beginning. Caught up in the stirrings of a mighty Waaagh!, Ghazghkull's hordes of Mekboyz began the construction of a veritable army of Stompas and Gargants, and as these colossal metal effigies rose higher, the tribes prepared for war.

THE WURLD KILLA

All this might have come to nothing had not Urk's sun started to flicker and die. Ghazghkull told the Ork tribes that this was a sign from Gork that the time had come to launch a Waaagh! bigger than any seen before. Those who wished to join the great crusade could follow Ghazghkull; those who disobeyed would die. To an Ork they chose to follow their prophet. They would conquer the galaxy or die in the attempt.

Fortuitously, some would say, a vast space hulk dropped out of the Warp at that moment and drifted in-system. Amid increasingly deadly radiation storms, Ghazghkull immediately declared the appearance of the vessel to be a gift from Gork and Mork, and ordered his Mekboyz to secure the space hulk, which they did using super-heavy traktor kannon and orbital harpoon platforms. Upon entering the ship, the Orks found the hulk already occupied, awash with daemonic entities. However, as Waaagh! Ghazghkull poured aboard in its billions, it swept deck after deck clear of Daemons with its overwhelming numbers. Speed Freeks roared through its vast cargo holds, duelling with droning swarms of gigantic daemonic flies. Vast mobs of Boyz and Nobz killed their way down the hulk's corridors under the terrifying leadership of the Mad Dok Grotsnik. A spearhead of Khornate Daemons poured from the heart of an ancient star freighter that was lodged amid the jumble of the hulk. Led by a towering daemonic Herald formed of flensed, blood-slick muscle, they attempted to split the Ork horde in two and cut them off from reinforcement. At this moment Ghazghkull himself stormed to the fore, shrugging off several grievous wounds as he closed on his foe. He backhanded the Khornate Herald's fiery blade from its fists, before pounding the mighty Daemon repeatedly into the deckplates with his power klaw. As more and more Orks flooded aboard the hulk, the last of the Daemons were banished back to the Immaterium, leaving the monolithic ship in Ork hands.

With the battle over, the space hulk began to move and headed once more out into the stars. For months, years or perhaps far longer the vast space hulk – which Ghazghkull had named *Wurld Killa* – lumbered through Warp space. It was far from an uneventful journey and the Orks were kept well occupied due to the taint of Chaos both within and without the vessel. Waaagh! Ghazghkull saw off several more minor daemonic incursions in this time, though gradually the attacks became less frequent, and soon the Ork tribes aboard *Wurld Killa* became increasingly restless.

WAR FOR ARMAGEDDON

Just as it looked as if its Ork passengers would turn upon one another, *Wurld Killa* plunged out of the Warp on the edge of the Armageddon system. Scattering defence platforms and panicked picket-ships from its path, Ghazghkull's hulk headed straight for Armageddon itself. Even as the Ork tribes on board began their final, frenzied preparations for war, *Wurld Killa* executed a terminal nosedive through Armageddon's atmosphere to crash-land on the continent of Armageddon Prime. Untold devastation was caused by the hulk's meteoric fall and hundreds of thousands of Orks were immolated during the atmospheric entry or killed upon impact, but these losses represented a mere fraction of the innumerable masses on board the colossal vessel.

In the wake of the Orks' apocalyptic arrival, Armageddon's defenders were left reeling. Even as the planetary defence force attempted to coordinate some form of response, billions upon billions of roaring greenskins poured from the dying carcass of *Wurld Killa*. They flooded out in an endless green tide, sweeping the scattered humans before them amid firestorms and dust-clouds so vast they could be seen by the horrified crews of the Imperial ships in orbit. Waaagh! Ghazghkull had arrived on Armageddon, and would visit utter carnage upon the world's luckless defenders in the days to come...

THE GREEN TIDE

The Orks have been a threat since before the earliest days of the Imperium, but the close of the 41st Millennium marks an unprecedented surge in greenskin activity. The galaxy trembles as a great Waaagh! echoes through the stars and beyond.

344.M41 TUSKA THE DAEMON-KILLA

Great Boss Tuska acquires a taste for fighting Daemons and makes straight for the Eye of Terror, a Waaagh! of like-minded lunatics gathering around him as he goes. Waaagh! Tuska proceeds to rampage across Daemon worlds beyond counting, before finally the eye of Khorne, the Blood God, turns upon them. Though overrun and slain by never-ending hordes of Daemons, Tuska's followers are transported to Khorne's own realm, there to fight for all eternity, reborn with each blood-soaked dawn to make war against Khorne's greatest daemonic generals for the Lord of Battles' amusement.

797.M41 GREEN TIDE OVER ULTIMA

The Ultima Segmentum is punished by wave after wave of greenskin uprisings and invasions. Numerous outlying worlds are overrun, and only the tireless efforts of Marneus Calgar and his Ultramarines prevent far greater destruction from occurring.

798.M41 WAAAGH! BIGSKORCHA

815.M41 THE WAR OF DAKKA

Warboss Grog Ironteef leads a mighty Waaagh! against the burgeoning Tau Empire, gathering up all the dakka he can to counter the firepower of his more advanced foes.

831.M41 WAAAGH! GAZBAG

Gazbag, a Speed Freek Warlord noted for his dogged determination if not his navigational skills, guides his Waaagh! toward a group of largely unprotected Eldar paradise worlds. The vengeful Eldar of Craftworld Biel-Tan descend upon the invaders with destructive fury, yet find the Orks a numerous and deadly foe. Eventually the Eldar are forced to withdraw, the flames of battle having reduced the paradise worlds' once verdant plains and jungles to smouldering ruins, providing Warboss Gazbag with a new empire to rule over.

837.M41 PORT SORCOL MASSACRE

844.M41 DANGER OVERLOOKED

On the world of Hephastine, Rogue Trader Maximillian Trusk discovers archeotech weapons from the Dark Age of Technology. Staving off attacks by the world's greenskin tribes, Trusk prepares to transport his prize to his awaiting fleet. However, a strikeforce under Lord Inquisitor Shael appears in orbit, demanding Trusk surrender the prescribed archeotech. When the Rogue Trader – who by now is staving off near constant attacks from an increasing number of Orks – refuses, Inquisitorial troops deploy to seize the weapons by force. As the fighting between the Rogue Trader's forces and Inquisitorial Storm Troopers escalates, more and more Orks are drawn in, scavenging weapons and soon becoming a rampaging horde. Yet both human factions continue more or less to ignore the greenskins, more interested in pursuing their own vendetta. After more than three months of warfare, Shael launches an all-out offensive against Trusk's fortified dig site, and even as the bitter rivals lock blades, the jungle rings to the deafening war cry of hundreds of thousands of Orks. From every direction, a tide of greenskins floods the compound, led by a vast Stompa that smashes its way through the defensive perimeter and charges headlong into the fight. Both Imperial factions are utterly annihilated, and the weapons over which they fought so hard are cannibalised for scrap.

855.M41 WAAAGH! HRUK

The noted Snakebites boss Hruk Teefsplinta enslaves the entire population of his old stomping grounds, the binary system Corva. Forcing his captives to build him spacecraft with holds cavernous enough to accommodate his beloved mega-menagerie, Hruk sets off for the core worlds of the Imperium. He conquers the nine shrine worlds of Marlisanct and uses the Basilica Imperator Majoris as a breeding pen for his famously incontinent Squiggoths.

862.M41 RALEPHOS OVERRUN

The great libraries on the archive world of Ralephos are overrun by a mighty Ork-led invasion. The greenskins burn everything, obliterating untold millennia of collected lore in a single night.

886.M41 HOPE'S END

Earth caste engineers of the Tau Ke'lshan Sept proudly reveal an immense new colony-seeding craft. This monolithic spacefaring vessel is named in the Tau language, *Hope's Light*. On its maiden voyage, and with over three hundred thousand Tau colonists and warriors on board, *Hope's Light* is boarded by the Ork fleet of Megaboss Morkrog and lost with all hands. For the next decade, the Ke'lshan Sept faces brutal raids from Morkrog's vast new looted warship *Taukilla*.

898.M41 THE MIGHTY MANGLER'S BATTLEWAGON BRIGADE

The Mighty Mangler of Bork launches his Waaagh! from the head of a vast brigade of Battlewagons. Each vehicle is incredibly well armoured, and the ground shakes when his brigade is on the move. To the dismay of the Imperial armies sent to intercept him, the Mighty Mangler lives up to his name. Waaagh! Bork collapses the defences of the Ghoul Stars and claims a great area of the galactic fringe.

907.M41 A GROWING THREAT

Segmentum commanders across the Imperium report an alarming upsurge in Ork activity. More Waaaghs! than ever before must be combatted.

925.M41 WAAAGH! GRAX

928.M41 THE THRASSOS DISASTER

Waaagh! Dregdakka ploughs headlong into the Adransa Cluster, causing untold devastation. On the planet of Thrassos a combined force of Space Marines from the Iron Knights and Liberators Chapters attempts to halt the Orks' steamroller advance. A horde of Orks including Dregdakka himself are lured onto a huge refinery platform before Techmarines destroy all bridges linking the platform to the mainland. Space Marine kill teams then deploy across the hulking structure, tasked with slaughtering the trapped greenskins and assassinating Dregdakka. Yet the Adeptus Astartes have woefully underestimated their foe, the greenskins digging in and fighting back with unexpected tenacity. Though they kill thousands of Orks, over three hundred Space Marines are slain and their comrades are overwhelmed as yet more Ork vessels pour into the system. His trophy poles rattling with freshly harvested Space Marine helmets, Warlord Dregdakka's position is now unassailable. His Waaagh! completely overruns the Adransa Cluster within the year.

934.M41 RISE OF THE WEIRDWAAAGH!

941.M41 THE SECOND WAR FOR ARMAGEDDON

Ghazghkull invades Armageddon at the head of a massive Ork Waaagh!. Only the vast miliary experience and leadership of Commissar Yarrick prevents the world from falling to the Orks within the first month of conflict. Space Marine reinforcements gradually turn the tide of the war and Ghazghkull retreats to the Golgotha sector to lick his wounds.

971.M41 WAAAGH! WAZDAKKA

976.M41 WAAAGH! GORBAG

977.M41 WAAAGH! PLANETSMASHA

Deathskulls Big Mek Fragrak da Planetsmasha vows he will surpass all other Deathskulls by looting an entire world, jerry-rigging a combination of traktor beams, ramships and city-sized rokkit boosters to push the third moon of Taurabrax out of its orbit, directly onto a collision course with its parent world. The resultant catastrophe renders all life on the thriving Imperial hive world extinct, fracturing continents, boiling the oceans off into space and burning away the world's atmosphere, finally reducing Taurabrax to a drifting debris field. Satisfied with his work, Big Mek Planetsmasha takes his pick of the choicest of these asteroids, adding thrusters, forcefields and ordnance arrays to turn them into a fleet of roks with which to spread even more mayhem across the system.

978.M41 THE LOST WAAAGH!

The Ork Warlord Grizgutz, a noted kleptomaniac, launches his Waaagh! into the Morloq system. Whilst using Warp travel to reach their quarry, Grizgutz and his warband unwittingly travel through time and emerge from the shifting chaos of the Empyrean shortly before they set off. Grizgutz hunts down and kills his doppelganger, reasoning that this way he can have a spare of his favourite gun. The resultant confusion stops the Waaagh! in its tracks.

978.M41 THE WURLDBREAKA BOMB

979.M41 A NEW WEAPON

Nazdreg, a Bad Moons Warlord noted for his wealth and flair, bullies his Meks into performing ever more progressive and bizarre experiments. Despite some nasty 'setbacks' ranging from spontaneous combustion to sporadic gravity reversal, Nazdreg's Meks perfect their tellyporta designs. The Warlord barters his new technology with Ghazghkull in exchange for an alliance.

979.M41 GRABORK'S BIG GUN

Big Mek Grabork and his mob of Meks salvage the space hulk *Perpetual Misery* from the depths of the void. Acting on instinct, Grabork and his Boyz set about pulling it apart and putting it back together into a new configuration, linking up dozens of ship reactors and cannibalizing hundreds of macro cannons to create a gargantuan shokk attack gun. Eager to try out his new weapon, the Big Mek attacks the world of Fratarn, raining petrified snotlings down upon the planet from orbit. However, when the snotlings run out, Grabork starts hurling Orks into the machine. Not liking the way things are going, one of Grabork's Meks turns the gun into reverse, sucking the entire world up into the *Perpetual Misery*. The resulting explosion obliterates the hulk and planet, and creates an asteroid field a billion miles across.

979.M41 WAAAGH! DREGFANG

980.M41 THE RIFTWAAAGH!

A new Warp anomaly blooms like a rancid flower in the Kantarak sector. Though the rift itself is small, the powerful emanations agitate indigenous greenskin populations throughout the sector. Driven wild, they launch Waaagh! after Waaagh! until Kantarak is reduced to war torn ruins.

981.M41 THE GREAT TITANHEIST

The forge world of Canto II is left badly weakened by a Tyranid splinter fleet, and the Blood Axes Warboss Mardrug sends a crack team of Kommandos and Mekboyz to steal the Warlord Titan *Wrath of Caseopea* amidst the chaos of the planet's recovery. The Kommandos shoot their way onboard the Titan, and their attendant Meks manage to jump-start its reactor. However, the Orks have no way of controlling the *Wrath of Caseopea*'s indignant machine spirit. Disoriented and enraged, the Titan goes on a devastating rampage across the planet before overloading its own reactor. The Kommandos' mission is a failure, but the devastation caused to a vital forge world is substantial, affecting supply to numerous Imperial war zones.

982.M41 Who's Da Boss?

During fierce fighting on the Exodite world of Lyrithar, Boss Zagstruk takes personal offence at being outmanoeuvred by the lightning-fast Wild Riders of Saim-Hann. Enraged beyond words as his cowardly foes retreat into the Webway, Zagstruk lights up his rokkit pack and gives chase along with a hard core of his most devoted Stormboyz. The portal closes behind Zagstruk, and Da Boss is next seen some ten months later when he stalks into the encampment of Warboss Golgrot. He slaughters a couple of dozen Lootas, and reclaims his stolen Fighta-Bommer. No-one has the guts to enquire as to Zagstruk's recent whereabouts, but all note the fresh batch of red and white Eldar helmets dangling from his belt.

982.M41 Troublesome Loot

Freebooter Dakbad Firegut lays claim to a vast living vessel he finds drifting in the void. The Ork pirates harpoon the creature, dragging it back to their base on great rusting chains. On the way, the bio-ship unleashes a horde of Tyranid creatures, Genestealers and Gaunts crawling up the chains to get at the Orks. Dakbad and his Boyz enjoy a lengthy game of target practice shooting the Tyranids off the chains using the kroozer's deck guns, until the Freebooter finally grows weary of the situation, unhooking the harpoons and leaving the bio-ship adrift on the edge of a densely populated Imperial system.

985.M41 Shyrrek's Folly

Archon Shyrrek of the Kabal of the Severed Hope seeks to turn the green hordes of Waaagh! Hammafist against the Tau Empire colony of Korvessa. Using hit and run attacks, Shyrrek's fleet lures the much larger Ork force toward Korvessa, but in their arrogance they underestimate the Orks completely. Using short range tellyporta drives, a number of Warlord Hammafist's kroozers leapfrog the Dark Eldar, leaving them surrounded and cut off from escape into the webway. Archon Shyrrek's forces fight like devils to escape the tightening ring of Ork ships. However their resistance comes to an end when Hammafist and his Meganob retinue tellyport on board Shyrrek's flagship and slice the Archon to shreds with their roaring killsaws.

986.M41 Ghesmengeist Overrun

987.M41: A Hundred, Hundred Teef

Waaagh! Ozdakka rampages through the Helshrike Systems, millions of Orks led by the legendary Bad Moon Boss of Bosses Ozdakka. Such is the utter destruction wrought by the Waaagh!, entire worlds being smashed to scrap and dragged off into the stars by the unstoppable Orks, that the Adeptus Terra dispatches a Vindicare Assassin to take out Ozdakka and his most powerful Nobz. Brutally effective,

the nameless assassin stalks the battlefields of Helshrike, sniping Orks from the shadows and taking a terrible toll on Ozdakka's bosses. In a fit of rage, the Warboss offers a hundred, hundred teef – more than most Orks can comprehend – for the head of the unseen killer. As word spreads of the bounty, even more Orks flock to Ozdakka's banner and his Waaagh! swells until it is even larger than ever. However, the Warboss does not live to enjoy the destruction he has wrought upon the Helshrike Sector, the assassin's final shot taking Ozdakka's head from his shoulders before the Imperial agent is overwhelmed by a mob of Bad Moons intent on claiming the immense prize.

989.M41 Waaagh! Snagrod

Snagrod, then Arch-Arsonist of Charadon, unites the Ork factions of the Loki sector. The nearby Imperial colony of Badlanding is destroyed despite a valiant defence at Krugerport. Intervention by the Crimson Fists Space Marines ensures that Snagrod's next target is the Adeptus Astartes planet of Rynn's World, where, after a titanic battle, the Crimson Fists' fortress monastery is atomised by a devastating explosion. The Orks are eventually driven off-world, but it is a hollow victory, for the once proud Crimson Fists are reduced to a fragment of their former glory.

989.M41 Waaagh! Blaktoof

994.M41 The March of Gork

A clanking mob of several hundred Gorkanauts sets out from the empire of Bork, beginning a destructive rampage that will become known as the March of Gork. From one world to the next, the lumbering machines smash everything in their path, the Meks building more Gorkanauts from every vehicle they destroy, until they are a nigh unstoppable tide of rusting metal.

995.M41 The Siege of Dorvenshold

996.M41 The Tide Rises Higher

Ork Waaaghs! reach epidemic levels across the Imperium. The forces of the Adeptus Astartes and Imperial Guard, already under incredible pressure from a multitude of threats, find themselves stretched thinner still as they are forced to respond to one Ork invasion after another. Many cannot be stopped, and countless worlds are overrun by the swarming masses of belligerent greenskins.

998.M41 The Third War for Armageddon

After five decades of planning and preparation, Ghazghkull returns to the barely recovered Imperial world at the head of an even greater Waaagh!, plunging Armageddon into another vast and bloody war. Yet after months of grinding conflict, the world has not fallen. As the Imperium commits vast reinforcements to War Zone Armageddon, countless waves of Orks flood to meet them and the war becomes a contest of grinding attrition with no end in sight.

DA GREAT WAAAGH!

The ripples of the Great Waaagh! are expanding throughout the galaxy. At their epicentre stands one Ork, the self-proclaimed prophet of Gork and Mork. Ghazghkull Mag Uruk Thraka claims to be guided by visions of the Ork gods, yet the incredible destruction he has wrought so far may be just the beginning.

990998.M41 A GREATER PURPOSE

Ghazghkull's visions become more frequent as his latest invasion of Armageddon drags on. They are now accompanied by blinding head pains and crackling green lights as Gork and Mork's roars of displeasure boom through Ghazghkull's mind. Leaving his generals to direct the war, Ghazghkull retreats to his command ship, *Kill Wrecka*, to brood. The Warlord surrounds himself with a mob of Warpheads, hoping the deranged Ork mystics can help to interpret his visions. Yet it is Ghazghkull himself who is finally struck by inspiration. He realises that no other Ork has his ambition. For the rest of the greenskin race, a good fight like Armageddon is enough to satisfy their bloodlust, but Ghazghkull can see beyond this to something greater. Possessed by a sudden, manic energy, the Warlord orders *Kill Wrecka* to break orbit. Scraping together a ragtag flotilla from whatever Ork warships are nearby, Ghazghkull makes for the edge of the system. He has no idea what he is searching for, only that it is not on Armageddon.

999998.M41 A DEADLY PURSUIT

Ghazghkull's departure does not go unmarked. Deep space auger-stations identify *Kill Wrecka* moving out of the Armageddon system. High Command are notified, and both Commissar Yarrick and High Marshal Helbrecht of the Black Templars elect to give chase. These heroes of the Imperium depart Armageddon some days later, leading every warship that can be spared. The Imperium allowed Ghazghkull to escape once and it cost them dearly. Yarrick vows the same mistake will not be made again.

189999.M41 THE BEAST AT BAY

Despite a sizeable headstart, Ghazghkull is tracked unerringly by his pursuers. The faster, more efficient Imperial Navy warships catch the Ork fleet several weeks after leaving Armageddon. In a dead region of space known as the Haunted Gulf, Ghazghkull's ships turn at bay for a last, desperate charge into the teeth of the Imperial Navy's guns. The void comes alight with lance beams and blazing broadsides as the Ork ships thunder into the midst of their foes, yet they stand little chance. Though they cripple several Imperial cruisers, the Ork ships are torn apart one by one. Yarrick and Helbrecht prepare to board *Kill Wrecka* and ensure Ghazghkull's demise once and for all. Yet even as they ready their assault, the ship is engulfed in a blaze of green energy and disappears without a trace.

189999.M41 GHAZGHKULL'S GREAT TASK

Even as his fleet is torn apart, Ghazghkull stomps around his bridge bellowing orders. The great Warlord is incandescent with fury, possessed of a vision so powerful that green lightning arcs around him. Their brains overwhelmed by this sudden surge of energy, his entourage of Warpheads convulse as one and begin to howl and gibber madly. As the crackling green energy that haloes Ghazghkull's skull lashes out to strike the Ork psykers, they are engulfed in green flames,

their eyes bursting and skin sizzling. With ectoplasmic power gushing from their maws, the Warpheads speak as one, their combined voice the mighty roar of Gork and Mork that Ghazghkull has heard all these months. Every Ork within earshot falls to their knees in awe as the gods tell Ghazghkull that this is not his time to die. They tell him that the whole galaxy must echo with the roar of the Ork. They charge Ghazghkull with gathering a Waaagh! like no other, the Waaagh! of Gork and Mork themselves. To do this, he must defeat every other Warlord, bring every last greenskin under his sway, and unite them all in a crusade that will drown the stars in war. Ghazghkull must unite this Great Waaagh!, and in so doing call forth Gork and Mork to lead the Boyz in a glorious battle that will last forever. Their message delivered, the Weirdboyz explode in ripe showers of wet viscera, and a tide of green power rolls outward from them, frying every system on Ghazghkull's ship and crippling his pursuers. *Kill Wrecka* is immediately hurled into Warp space, emerging somewhere (and somewhen) else entirely.

694999.M41 DA GREAT WAAAGH!

Kill Wrecka drops out of the Warp in the midst of the sprawling territory controlled by Ork Warlord Urgok Da Slayer. Ghazghkull is revitalised, red eyes blazing with new purpose. *Kill Wrecka* makes straight for Urgok's mighty space fortress. Knowing his only advantage is surprise, Ghazghkull fires up his ship's tellyporta, transporting himself and a mob of his baddest Nobz in a roaring blast of light, directly into Urgok's throne room. Urgok looks on in horror as Ghazghkull tears through his bodyguards as though they were rowdy grots. Then, trampling over their mangled corpses with his shoota still smoking, Ghazghkull looms over his cowed rival and 'invites' him to join Da Great Waaagh!.

Most of Urgok's Boyz join the Waaagh! willingly, while those too slow to spot which way the wind is howling are quickly beaten into submission. Within weeks, news of Ghazghkull's new Waaagh! spreads far and wide, the massive Warboss' legend reaching the ears of Orks hundreds of light years away, sparking the first stirring of an Ork migration on a scale never seen before. With a whole new Waaagh! at his disposal and Urgok his personal toadie, Ghazghkull turns his attentions to the galactic southeast and the empire of Octarius. If the whole galaxy is going to be engulfed in war, Gork and Mork will need a lot more Orks for their Great Waaagh! Besides, Ghazghkull has decided to show the Ork ruler of Octarius what a real Overfiend looks like...

ORK WARBANDS

An Ork army gathered for war is an impressive sight, particularly when, as with the Split-Grin Bad Moon tribe shown here, its warriors are drawn from the same clan and bear the same colours and iconography.

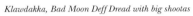
Klawdakka, Bad Moon Deff Dread with big shootas

Grimskar, Bad Moon Meganob

Nazgrek Steeleye, Bad Moon Big Mek with tellyport blasta

Drokk Goldfist, Bad Moon Meganob

Krank, Bad Moon Big Mek with shokk attack gun

Bad Moon Boyz advance with guns blazing, their tribe's Gorkanauts lumbering in support.

Morgob, Bad Moon Nob

'Bullseye' Bogrok, Bad Moon Boy with rokkit launcha

Kutrag, Bad Moon Painboy

Deffdroppa, Bad Moon Blitza-bommer

Kaptin Badrukk, da Freeboota King

Da Bragga Boyz, Flash Gitz

Smilin' Grogg's Flash Gitz

Kaptin Dakbad

FORCES OF THE ORKS

The following section details background and rules information that describe the forces used by the Orks – their warriors, their vehicles and the characters that lead them to battle. This section will enable you to forge your collection of Ork miniatures into an army ready to fight battles in your games of Warhammer 40,000.

DATASHEETS

Each Ork unit in this book has a datasheet. These detail either Army List Entries or Formations, providing all the rules information that you will need to use your models in your games of Warhammer 40,000.

ARMY LIST ENTRIES

Each Army List Entry contains the following information:

1 **Faction:** *The unit's Faction is shown here by a symbol. All units that have this symbol, which is all the units described in this book, have the Orks Faction.*

2 **Battlefield Role:** *The unit's Battlefield Role is shown here by a symbol. Units in this book have one of the following Battlefield Roles: HQ, Troops, Elites, Fast Attack, Heavy Support and Lords of War. The symbols for these battlefield roles are defined in Warhammer 40,000: The Rules.*

3 **Unit Name:** *Here you will find the name of the unit.*

4 **Unit Description:** *This section provides a background description of the unit, detailing their particular strengths and weaknesses along with the tactics and methods they employ to wage war in the grim darkness of the 41st Millennium.*

5 **Points Cost:** *This is the points cost of the unit without any upgrades, used if you are choosing an army to a points value.*

6 **Unit Profile:** *This section will show the profiles of any models the unit can include.*

7 **Unit Type:** *This refers to the unit type rules in Warhammer 40,000: The Rules. For example, a unit may be classed as Infantry, Cavalry or Vehicle, which will subject it to a number of rules regarding movement, shooting, assaults, etc.*

8 **Unit Composition:** *This section will show the number and type of models that make up the basic unit, before any upgrades have been taken.*

9 **Wargear:** *This section details the weapons and equipment the models in the unit are armed with, many of which are described in more detail in the Appendix section of this book. The cost for all the unit's basic equipment is included in its points cost.*

10 **Special Rules:** *Any special rules that apply to models in the unit are listed here. Special rules that are unique to models in that unit are described in full here, whilst others are detailed either in the Appendix section of this book (pg 92) or in the Special Rules section of Warhammer 40,000: The Rules.*

11 **Options:** *This section lists all of the upgrades you may add to the unit if you wish to do so, alongside the associated points cost for each. Where an option states that you may exchange one weapon*

'and/or' another, you may replace either or both, provided you pay the points cost for each. The abbreviation 'pts' stands for 'points' and 'pts/model' stands for 'points per model'. Where applicable, this section also refers to any Transports the unit may take. These have their own datasheets. Dedicated Transports do not use up any slots on a Force Organisation Chart, but otherwise function as separate units. The Detachments section of Warhammer 40,000: The Rules explains how Dedicated Transports work.

12 **Warlord Traits:** *Sometimes a character's datasheet will have a specific Warlord Trait, in which case it will be listed here.*

13 **Gifts of Gork and Mork:** *Some entries have unique items of wargear, the description and rules for which will be listed here.*

FORMATIONS

Formation datasheets are identified by this symbol. The rules for Formations can be found in *Warhammer 40,000: The Rules*. A Formation datasheet will list the Army List Entries which make up the Formation, any restrictions upon what it may include, and any special rules the Formation's units gain.

ORKS WARGEAR LIST

These lists detail the points values of various items of wargear available to units in your army. Many unit entries in the datasheets that follow may include wargear options from one or more of these lists – in each instance, the datasheet will tell you (in bold text) exactly which of these lists you may use. Rules for these items can be found in the Appendix (pg 92).

Ranged Weapons .... pg 94
A model may replace its ranged weapon with one of the following:
- Shoota .... *free*
- Twin-linked shoota .... *3 pts*
- Kombi-weapon with rokkit launcha .... *5 pts*
- Kombi-weapon with skorcha .... *10 pts*

Melee Weapons .... pg 93
A model may replace its melee weapon with one of the following:
- Big choppa .... *5 pts*
- Power klaw .... *25 pts*

Mek Weapons .... pg 94
A model can replace their ranged weapon with one of the following:
- Kombi-weapon with rokkit launcha .... *5 pts*
- Kustom mega-blasta .... *5 pts*
- Rokkit launcha .... *5 pts*
- Kombi-weapon with skorcha .... *10 pts*
- Kustom mega-slugga .... *10 pts*

Runts & Squigs .... pg 97
A model can take any combination of the following:
- 0-3 Ammo runts .... *3 pts each*
- 0-3 Grot oilers [1] .... *5 pts each*
- 0-1 Grot orderly [2] .... *5 pts*
- 0-1 Attack squig .... *15 pts*

Orky Know-wots .... pg 98
A model can take up to one of each of the following:
- Bosspole .... *5 pts*
- Cybork body .... *5 pts*
- Gitfinda .... *5 pts*
- Warbike [3] .... *25 pts*

Gifts of Gork and Mork .... pg 100
Only one of each of the following may be taken per army. A model can take one of the following:
- Da Dead Shiny Shoota .... *5 pts*
- Da Finkin' Kap [4] .... *10 pts*
- Da Fixer Upperz [1] .... *15 pts*
- Da Lucky Stikk .... *25 pts*
- Headwoppa's Killchoppa .... *20 pts*
- Warboss Gazbag's Blitzbike [3] .... *35 pts*

Ork Vehicle Equipment .... pg 99
A model can take up to one of each of the following:
- Red paint job .... *5 pts*
- Reinforced ram [5] .... *5 pts*
- Stikkbomb chukka .... *5 pts*
- Extra armour .... *10 pts*
- Grot riggers .... *10 pts*
- Wreckin' ball .... *10 pts*
- Boarding plank .... *15 pts*

[1] *Meks and Big Meks only.*
[2] *Painboyz only.*
[3] *Cannot be taken by a model with mega armour.*
[4] *Can only be taken by your Warlord.*
[5] *Cannot be taken by a vehicle with a deff rolla.*

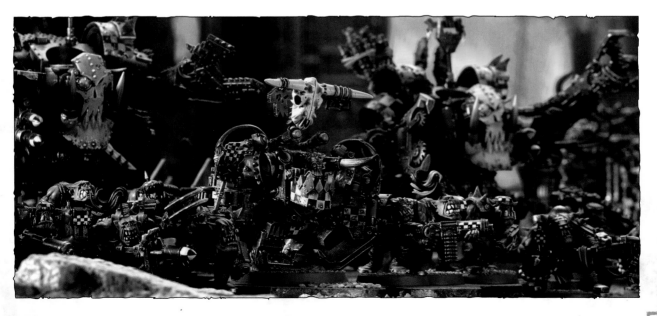

WARBOSS

An Ork Warboss is the strongest, toughest, loudest and most violent Ork in his tribe. These massive greenskins seize the lion's share of the loot from every fight, meaning they are usually armed and armoured better than any of their followers. Warbosses are not above making a swift and messy example of anyone whose kit seems shinier or more killy than theirs. They wield absolute authority over their tribe, for greenskin society is based on the idea that might makes right. While some Warbosses show glimmerings of intelligence, all are at their best when busting heads and bellowing until things are done their way. A Warboss will generally be able to get the ladz to battle in some semblance of order, but strategy and tactical thinking aren't usually their strong suits. Rather, a Warboss is a mountain of muscle and violence who will invariably lead from the front, rampaging through the enemy ranks with shoota blazing and power klaw swinging wildly. Especially successful Warbosses will continue to grow in both stature and power with every war they win. Eventually, the greatest of them will come to lead a Waaagh! of apocalyptic size. All other races dread the rise of such a Warlord, for he will command a horde capable of drowning whole systems in war and causing the deaths of billions.

	WS	BS	S	T	W	I	A	Ld	Sv	Unit Type	Unit Composition
Warboss	5	2	5	5	3	4	4	9	6+	Infantry (Character)	1 Warboss

WARGEAR:
- **Slugga** (pg 96)
- **Choppa** (pg 93)
- **Stikkbombs** (pg 98)

SPECIAL RULES:
- **'Ere We Go!** (pg 92)
- **Furious Charge**
- **Independent Character**
- **Mob Rule** (pg 92)

Waaagh!: Once per game, at the start of any of your turns after the first, a model with this special rule can, if he is your Warlord, call a Waaagh! On the turn he does so, all friendly units made up entirely of models with the 'Ere We Go! special rule may charge in the Assault phase even if they made a Run move in the same turn.

OPTIONS:
- May take 'eavy armour .... 4 pts
- May replace slugga and choppa with mega armour, twin-linked shoota and power klaw .... 40 pts
- May take items from the **Ranged Weapons, Melee Weapons, Runts & Squigs, Orky Know-wots** and/or **Gifts of Gork and Mork** lists.

WEIRDBOY

Weirdboyz are the most psychically attuned of all Orks. They are capable of vomiting blasts of Warp energy that can reduce foes to molten goop in seconds. Weirdboyz unconsciously channel the background mental emissions of nearby greenskins. Even a close-run squig-eating contest between two rowdy Boyz will cause waves of energy to pulse through any Weirdboy that strays near. Unless the Weirdboy finds some way to release this pent-up energy his head will explode, detonating the heads of nearby Orks into the bargain. This can prove highly inconvenient. Any Weirdboy lucky enough to reach maturity will have learned how to release his powers in a searing energy blast or destructive wave. Though this makes the Weirdboy feel fantastic, it can result in a messy death for anyone in his vicinity. Some Weirdboyz, known as Warpheads, become addicted to the thrill of spewing Waaagh! energy, actively seeking out the deadly rush of battle. However, for most Weirdboyz the battlefield is a miserable and dangerous place. They must normally be dragged there by burly minders, pointed unceremoniously at the foe, and forced to spew mighty bolts of ectoplasmic energy in their general direction. This affords the Weirdboy a few moments of blissful relief before the whole process begins again.

	WS	BS	S	T	W	I	A	Ld	Sv	Unit Type	Unit Composition
Weirdboy	4	2	4	4	2	3	3	7	6+	Infantry (Character)	1 Weirdboy

WARGEAR:
- Weirdboy staff (pg 93)

SPECIAL RULES:
- 'Ere We Go! (pg 92)
- Furious Charge
- Independent Character
- Mob Rule (pg 92)
- Psyker (Mastery Level 1)

Waaagh! Energy: A Weirdboy generates a bonus +1 Warp Charge point if, at the start of your Psychic phase, there are ten or more models with the 'Ere We Go! special rule within 12" of him. If a Weirdboy generates a bonus Warp Charge point in this manner, he must pass at least one Psychic test during that phase or suffer a single Strength 2 hit at the end of that Psychic phase with no saves allowed. This special rule does not apply if the Weirdboy is embarked inside a Transport or Building.

PSYKER: Weirdboyz generate their powers from the **Power of the Waaagh!** and **Daemonology** disciplines.

OPTIONS:
- May be upgraded to Psyker (Mastery Level 2) .... 25 pts

MEK

Ork Meks go to war festooned in clanking, smoke-belching contraptions of their own design. These eccentric inventions confound friend and foe alike, as their purpose often remains a mystery until the big red button gets pushed. When triggered, a Mek's latest invention might fire blasts of energy that immolate swathes of the enemy, or project wobbling bubbles of force to protect nearby Boyz from harm. On the other hand, it might belch showers of sparks before engulfing its operator and everyone nearby in a roiling ball of flame. Yet occasional malfunctions are forgiven by the Orks, for even when a Mekboy's temperamental new wotsit does decide to explode, at least it gives the Boyz a good laugh. Without Mekboyz, Orks would lack for light, power, transport, and even guns (they lack for sanitation regardless, but that's another story). Whenever an Ork needs something building, be it a shiny new shoota or the boss' new ride, they go straight to the Meks. Furthermore, an Ork with teef to spare will take existing kit to the nearest Mek in the hope of having damage repaired, and maybe some kustomising done. It is a rare day that the customer gets what he asked for, but whatever the Mek turns out will normally be fairly flash all the same.

	WS	BS	S	T	W	I	A	Ld	Sv	Unit Type	Unit Composition
Mek	4	2	3	4	1	2	2	7	6+	Infantry (Character)	1 Mek

WARGEAR:
- Slugga (pg 96)
- Choppa (pg 93)
- Mek's tools (pg 98)
- Stikkbombs (pg 98)

SPECIAL RULES:
- 'Ere We Go! (pg 92)
- Furious Charge
- Mob Rule (pg 92)

Mekaniaks: For each HQ choice in a detachment (not including other Meks) you may include a single Mek chosen from this datasheet. These selections do not use up Force Organisation slots. Before the battle, immediately after determining Warlord Traits, any Mek that is not already part of another unit must, if possible, be assigned to any unit with the Infantry or Artillery type in their detachment; a Mek cannot leave his unit and is treated as part of it for the entire battle for all rules purposes.

OPTIONS:
- Any Mek may replace his choppa with a killsaw......................30 pts
- Any Mek may be accompanied by a grot oiler..5 pts
- Any Mek may take items from the **Mek Weapons** list.

BIG MEK

Especially talented or popular Mekboyz will soon attract a following, lording it over a growing gang of underlings. A Mek with this much clout is referred to as a Big Mek, and can prove indispensable to the local Warboss with his knowledge of shokk attack guns, force field technology, and tellyporta rigs. Yet Warbosses don't willingly suffer rivals. If a Big Mek gets too big for his boots, he will soon find himself at the business end of a very large gun (probably the one he built for the boss a couple of weeks earlier). In such circumstances, most Big Meks will choose exile. Such freebooter Big Meks either wind up hiring out their skills to a new tribe, or else building their very own Warband replete with clanking, roaring walkers, seething mobs of Lootas and Burna Boyz, and ramshackle masses of wagons and artillery.

	WS	BS	S	T	W	I	A	Ld	Sv	Unit Type	Unit Composition
Big Mek	4	2	4	4	2	3	3	8	6+	Infantry (Character)	1 Big Mek

WARGEAR:
- **Slugga** (pg 96)
- **Choppa** (pg 93)
- **Mek's tools** (pg 98)
- **Stikkbombs** (pg 98)

SPECIAL RULES:
- **'Ere We Go!** (pg 92)
- **Furious Charge**
- **Independent Character**
- **Mob Rule** (pg 92)

OPTIONS:
- A Big Mek may take 'eavy armour .... *4 pts*
- A Big Mek may replace his slugga with one of the following:
  - Kustom force field .... *50 pts*
  - Shokk attack gun .... *50 pts*
- A Big Mek may replace his choppa with a killsaw .... *30 pts*
- A Big Mek may take items from the **Mek Weapons, Melee Weapons, Runts & Squigs, Orky Know-wots** and/or **Gifts of Gork and Mork** lists.
- A Big Mek may replace his slugga and choppa with mega armour, kustom mega-blasta and power klaw .... *40 pts*
- A Big Mek with mega armour may take items from the **Ranged Weapons, Runts & Squigs, Orky Know-wots** and/or **Gifts of Gork and Mork** lists.
- A Big Mek with mega armour can replace his kustom mega-blasta with a killsaw .... *10 pts*
- A Big Mek with mega armour can take one of the following
  - Tellyport blasta .... *25 pts*
  - Kustom force field .... *50 pts*

PAINBOY

50 POINTS

Often referred to by other Orks as Doks, Painboyz are the greenskin equivalent of both surgeons and dentists. They are driven to perform exploratory surgery on living creatures just as Mekboyz are driven to fiddle with machinery. Devious, deranged, and usually covered in gore from head to toe, Painboyz are a menace to friend and foe alike. This is never truer than when a Painboy finds an opponent between him and a fallen Ork with a gobful of unclaimed teef. Painboyz are at home amid the blood and horror of the battlefield. Between the screaming, the jetting gore, and the liberally smeared filth, such conditions tend to remind them fondly of their operating theatres. These sadistic butchers grin through every crunch, squelch and spurt as they ply their trade amid the fires of battle. Painboyz prefer their victims conscious so they can make sure they're still alive. Yet Ork physiology is incredibly durable, their pain threshold high enough that all but the most grievously invasive procedures can be survived. Painboyz' brutal liberties are normally overlooked, especially when a Dok successfully re-staples a prominent Nob's head mid-battle, or furnishes the Warboss with a brand new flame-throwing arm.

	WS	BS	S	T	W	I	A	Ld	Sv	Unit Type	Unit Composition
Painboy	4	2	4	4	2	3	3	7	6+	Infantry (Character)	1 Painboy

WARGEAR:
- **'Urty syringe** (pg 93)
- **Dok's tools** (pg 98)

SPECIAL RULES:
- **'Ere We Go!** (pg 92)
- **Furious Charge**
- **Independent Character**
- **Mob Rule** (pg 92)

OPTIONS:
- A Painboy may take items from the **Orky Know-wots** and/or **Runts & Squigs** lists.

> 'ORKSES NEVER LOSE A BATTLE. IF WE WIN WE WIN, IF WE DIE WE DIE FIGHTIN' SO IT DON'T COUNT. IF WE RUNS FOR IT WE DON'T DIE NEITHER, COS WE CAN COME BACK FOR ANNUVER GO, SEE!'
>
> - Commonly held Ork view of warfare

MAD DOK GROTSNIK
DA PAINBOSS

160 POINTS

Mad Dok Grotsnik is an absolute terror, the most bloodthirsty and deranged of an unhinged breed. Once a Painboy of some skill, Grotsnik is now all but berserk with the desire to do harm to others. Raving and screaming, the delusional Dok leads the charge toward the foe at an all-out sprint, unmindful of enemy fire in his desperation to sink needles and blades into unwilling flesh. His surgical skills are questionable at best, and only the most desperate will go to him for medical assistance. Yet Ghazghkull will tolerate no threat to the safety of the Ork who facilitated his visions. Indeed, as Ghazghkull's Great Waaagh! blazes its way across the stars, Grotsnik has become an integral part of the Goff Warlord's personal retinue. The Dok has not entirely lost his touch with a chain-scalpel – for some reason he still seems able to rein in his maddened impulses if ever called upon to tend the wounds of Ghazghkull himself, and has saved the mighty warlord's life on more than one occasion. Otherwise, however, Grotsnik's chief value these days is as a fighter. He is as brutal as the meanest Goff Nob, and his sheer boundless ferocity serves him well in the press of battle. Here, the Dok becomes a frenzied whirlwind, his excesses inspiring those Orks around him to ever-greater acts of violence.

	WS	BS	S	T	W	I	A	Ld	Sv	Unit Type	Unit Composition
Mad Dok Grotsnik	5	2	4	5	3	3	4	9	4+	Infantry (Character)	1 (Unique)

WARGEAR:
- **Slugga** (pg 96)
- **Power klaw** (pg 93)
- **Dok's tools** (pg 98)
- **'Urty syringe** (pg 93)
- **Cybork body** (pg 98)

WARLORD TRAIT:
- **Brutal but Kunnin'** (pg 92)

SPECIAL RULES:
- **'Ere We Go!** (pg 92)
- **Furious Charge**
- **Independent Character**
- **Mob Rule** (pg 92)

One Scalpel Short of a Medpack: Dok Grotsnik and any unit he joins have the Fearless and Rampage special rules. Once Dok Grotsnik has joined a unit, he may not leave it unless he is the last remaining member of that unit.

KAPTIN BADRUKK
DA FREEBOOTA KING

Kaptin Badrukk is the greatest Flash Git there ever was. He is ostentatious in the extreme – his heavily scarred and tattooed head is decorated with medals taken from defeated Imperial admirals whose ships he has ransacked. His teeth, so numerous that Badrukk's face is permanently split by a hideous rictus grin, are plated with an alloy of adamantium and priceless ur-gold stolen from the Palace of Undying Light. The Kaptin's gilded armour is polished to a greasy sheen, and his back banners proclaim his supreme abilities as a fighter. A lead-lined greatcoat protects Badrukk from the radiation generated by his beloved weapon, Da Rippa, a gun so dangerous that merely standing near it is tantamount to a death sentence. For an Ork, Badrukk is an excellent strategist, and acts as an advisor for any Warlord rich enough to meet his exorbitant fees. After the battle, Badrukk usually 'persuades' his employers to hand over the lion's share of the booty before departing in Da Blacktoof in search of more carnage. Many Warlords see this as a price well worth paying for the unforgettable sight of Badrukk's Flash Gitz unleashing their deadly guns upon the foe.

	WS	BS	S	T	W	I	A	Ld	Sv	Unit Type	Unit Composition
Kaptin Badrukk	5	2	4	4	2	3	4	9	3+	Infantry (Character)	1 (Unique)

WARGEAR:
- **Slugga** (pg 96)
- **Choppa** (pg 93)
- **Stikkbombs** (pg 98)
- **Bosspole** (pg 98)
- **Gitfinda** (pg 98)

WARLORD TRAIT:
- **Kunnin' but Brutal** (pg 92)

SPECIAL RULES:
- **'Ere We Go!** (pg 92)
- **Furious Charge**
- **Independent Character**
- **Mob Rule** (pg 92)

OPTIONS:
- Take up to 3 ammo runts........... *3 pts each*

GIFTS OF GORK AND MORK

Goldtoof Armour: *Kaptin Badrukk's priceless war-plate is fashioned from looted power armour, and houses a miniature force field generator.*

Goldtoof armour confers a 3+ Armour Save and a 5+ invulnerable save.

Da Rippa: *This gun once belonged to the Ogryn bodyguard of a sub-sector governor. The Kaptin has since had it kustomised to fire unstable plasma canisters instead of extreme-calibre bullets.*

Range	S	AP	Type
24"	7	2	Assault 3, Gets Hot

BOSS ZAGSTRUK
DA BOSS

Boss Zagstruk is one of the most shockingly violent Orks in the galaxy. He is perpetually angry, and his bulge-eyed glare is enough to subdue even the most raucous Madboy. His approach is heralded by the metallic quickstep clank of his bionik legs, sending every grot within earshot skulking. Some claim that Zagstruk once stared down a rampaging bull Squiggoth, though others reckon it more likely that he simply clobbered the bellowing beast until it keeled over senseless. Zagstruk is a ferocious disciplinarian with absolutely no tolerance for stupidity, incompetence or failure. He is more than happy to put a few rounds through the skull of any greenskin who displays such traits around him, a fact that tends to keep even the biggest and most truculent Orks in line. Known simply as 'Da Boss' by the awed Stormboyz who flock to his banner, Zagstruk's thermonuclear temper is legend. He never lowers his voice below a bellow, and can fly into a murderous rage with no provocation whatsoever. The rumour is that Zagstruk has never gone a day without killing something. Da Boss inspires fanatical awe in the Stormboyz who queue up to fight alongside him, and for every underling that he shoots dead there are always two new recruits ready to join the ranks.

	WS	BS	S	T	W	I	A	Ld	Sv	Unit Type	Unit Composition
Boss Zagstruk	5	2	5	4	2	3	4	8	4+	Jump Infantry (Character)	1 (Unique)

WARGEAR:
- **Slugga** (pg 96)
- **Choppa** (pg 93)
- **'Eavy armour** (pg 99)
- **Stikkbombs** (pg 98)
- **Cybork body** (pg 98)
- **Rokkit pack** (pg 98)

WARLORD TRAIT:
- **Bellowing Tyrant** (pg 92)

SPECIAL RULES:
- **'Ere We Go!** (pg 92)
- **Furious Charge**
- **Independent Character**
- **Mob Rule** (pg 92)

GIFTS OF GORK AND MORK
Da Vulcha's Klaws: *Da Vulcha's Klaws were made for Zagstruk after his legs were ripped off by a Space Marine Dreadnought. These piston-driven and power-clawed augmetics ensure that when the Boss makes contact with the enemy it is always with a sickening crunch.*

Hammer of Wrath attacks made by Boss Zagstruk are Strength 8 and AP2.

Ork Boyz are the heart and soul of any warband. They charge into battle in a great mass, crashing into the enemy like a green landslide. Bellowing with the joy of battle, mobs of Ork Boyz excel at close quarters where they can hack, bludgeon and stamp their foes into bloody ruin. The average Ork Boy is mean-tempered and exceptionally tough, more than compensating for his lack of intellect with a talent for violence. Though an Ork can cause plenty of damage with his fists, feet and forehead, it takes a lot to separate one from his favourite choppa. When it comes to firearms, Orks love simplicity. They value noise and sheer weight of fire though so long as a gun can double as a decent club, its owner is usually happy enough. Some greenskins will even get their hands on crude heavy weapons with which they can cause absolute havoc.

	WS	BS	S	T	W	I	A	Ld	Sv	Unit Type	Unit Composition
Ork Boy	4	2	3	4	1	2	2	7	6+	Infantry	10 Ork Boyz
Boss Nob	4	2	4	4	2	3	3	7	6+	Infantry (Character)	

WARGEAR:
- **Slugga** (pg 96)
- **Choppa** (pg 93)
- **Stikkbombs** (pg 98)

SPECIAL RULES:
- **'Ere We Go!** (pg 92)
- **Furious Charge**
- **Mob Rule** (pg 92)

OPTIONS:
- May include up to twenty additional Ork Boyz .... 6 pts/model
- The entire mob may replace their sluggas
  with shootas .... 1 pt/model
- The entire mob may take 'eavy armour .... 4 pts/model
- For every ten models in the unit, one Ork Boy may replace
  their ranged weapon with one of the following:
  - Big shoota .... 5 pts
  - Rokkit launcha .... 5 pts
- One other model may be upgraded to a Boss Nob .... 10 pts
- The Boss Nob may take items from the **Ranged Weapons** and/or **Melee Weapons** lists.
- The Boss Nob may take a bosspole .... 5 pts
- The unit may select a Trukk as a Dedicated Transport (pg 70).

GRETCHIN

Gretchin – or grots – flood across the battlefield in great squabbling mobs. Individually feeble and cowardly, grots can nonetheless prove surprisingly dangerous in large numbers. Herded squealing toward the foe by the irascible old bullies known as Runtherds, the tiny greenskins are made to fight tooth and claw for their pitiful lives. When forced to fight or die, a sizeable mob of grots can overrun even a well-prepared foe, clawing and biting frantically in their desperation to stay alive. Though not especially dangerous up close, the average Gretchin is more than capable of out-shooting his Ork masters. This talent goes largely to waste, of course, as no self-respecting Ork is going to let some runty grot strut about with a decent shoota. However, a massed volley with their so-called grot blastas can cause a surprising amount of bloodshed.

	WS	BS	S	T	W	I	A	Ld	Sv	Unit Type	Unit Composition
Gretchin	2	3	2	2	1	2	1	5	-	Infantry	10 Gretchin
Runtherd	4	2	3	4	1	2	2	7	6+	Infantry (Character)	1 Runtherd

WARGEAR:

Gretchin:
• **Grot blasta** (pg 95)

Runtherd:
• **Grabba stikk** (pg 93)
• **Slugga** (pg 96)
• **Stikkbombs** (pg 98)

SPECIAL RULES:
• **'Ere We Go!**
  (Runtherd only) (pg 92)
• **Furious Charge**
  (Runtherd only)

OPTIONS:
• May include up to twenty additional Gretchin ...... *3 pts/model*
• Must take one additional Runtherd for every 10 additional Gretchin in the unit .... *10 pts/model*
• Any Runtherd may replace their grabba stikk with a grot-prod .... *5 pts/model*
• Any Runtherd may take a squig hound .... *5 pts/model*

BURNA BOYZ

Burna Boyz are dedicated arsonists all, advancing on the foe amid gouts of billowing flame. They love nothing more than burning other peoples' stuff, and the owners too if they can get them. These lunatics will set light to anything or anyone for the simple joy of watching them 'do the burny dance'. They can prove utterly lethal to tightly packed or lightly armoured infantry, the roiling blasts of their burnas flushing their victims out of cover amid the sizzle of cooking flesh. Faced with more heavily armoured enemies, the Burna Boyz simply twist the apertures of their burnas to provide a tight, metal-slicing jet of blue heat. Charging into combat, Burna Boyz use these weapons to slice even incredibly resilient foes into glowing, heat-seared chunks.

	WS	BS	S	T	W	I	A	Ld	Sv	Unit Type	Unit Composition
Burna Boy	4	2	3	4	1	2	2	7	6+	Infantry	5 Burna Boyz
Mek	4	2	3	4	1	2	2	7	6+	Infantry (Character)	

WARGEAR:
- **Burna** (pg 94)
- **Stikkbombs** (pg 98)

SPECIAL RULES:
- **'Ere We Go!** (pg 92)
- **Furious Charge**
- **Mob Rule** (pg 92)

OPTIONS:
- May include up to ten additional Burna Boyz...... *16 pts/model*
- Up to three models may be upgraded to Meks, replacing their burnas with Mek's tools, slugga and choppa...*free*
- Any Mek may be accompanied by a grot oiler........ *5 pts/model*
- Any Mek may replace his choppa with a killsaw... *20 pts/model*
- Any Mek can take items from the **Mek Weapons** list.
- The unit may select a Trukk as a Dedicated Transport (pg 70).

'OOMANS ARE PINK AND SOFT, NOT TOUGH AND GREEN LIKE DA BOYZ. THEY'Z ALL DA SAME SIZE TOO, SO THEY'Z ALWAYS ARGUING ABOUT WHO'S IN CHARGE, COS THERE'S NO WAY OF TELLIN' 'CEPT FER BADGES AND OONIFORMS AND FINGS. WHEN ONE OF 'EM WANTS TO LORD IT OVER DA UVVERS, HE SAYS, 'I'M VERY SPESHUL SO YOU GOTTA WORSHIP ME,' OR 'I KNOW SUMMINK WOT YOU LOT DON'T KNOW, SO YER BETTER LISTEN GOOD'. DA FUNNY FING IS, ARF OF 'EM BELIEVE IT AND DA UVVER ARF DON'T, SO 'E 'AS TO HIT 'EM ALL ANYWAY OR RUN FER IT. WOT A LOT OF MUKKIN' ABOUT IF YOU ASKS ME. AN' WHILE THEY'Z ALL ARGUIN' WIV EACH UVVER OVER WHO'S DA BOSS, DA ORKS CAN CLOBBER DA LOT.'

- An Ork Boy's view of Humanity and its failings

TANKBUSTAS

Tankbustas are Orks who have become completely addicted to the thrill of destroying the armoured fighting vehicles of their foes. Their desire to hunt down and slay the biggest, most dangerous tanks they can find echoes the primal instinct of the big game hunter. Indeed, as primitive hunters might claim a gruesome trophy from a fallen beast to better brag of its demise, so Tankbustas will strip the choicest loot from the wreckage of a ruined tank. Colourful hull plates are hammered into crude armour, internal gubbins worn proudly as warrior jewellery, and the flayed skins of crewmen are draped round the Tankbustas' shoulders like pelts. They equip themselves extensively for dealing death to enemy armour – their whistling volleys of rokkits, and lethal tankbusta bomb assaults can spell annihilation for even the heaviest tanks.

	WS	BS	S	T	W	I	A	Ld	Sv	Unit Type	Unit Composition
Tankbusta	4	2	3	4	1	2	2	7	6+	Infantry	5 Tankbustas
Boss Nob	4	2	4	4	2	3	3	7	6+	Infantry (Character)	

WARGEAR:
- **Rokkit launcha** (pg 95)
- **Stikkbombs** (pg 98)
- **Tankbusta bombs** (pg 98)

SPECIAL RULES:
- **'Ere We Go!** (pg 92)
- **Furious Charge**
- **Mob Rule** (pg 92)
- **Tank Hunters**

Glory Hogs: In a mission that has the First Blood Secondary Objective, the Ork player receives double the normal number of Victory Points from that objective if the first casualty to be removed is an enemy vehicle that was destroyed by an attack made by one or more units of Tankbustas.

OPTIONS:
- May include up to ten additional Tankbustas....... *13 pts/model*
- May include up to three bomb squigs..................... *5 pts/model*
- Up to two Tankbustas may replace their rokkit launchas with tankhammers .... *15 pts/model*
- One model may be upgraded to a Boss Nob .... *10 pts*
- The Boss Nob may take items from the **Melee Weapons** list.
- The Boss Nob may take a bosspole..................................... *5 pts*
- The unit may select a Trukk as a Dedicated Transport (pg 64).

NOBZ

Second in status only to the Warboss, Ork Nobz are big, bad and brutal. Serving as a crude greenskin ruling class, the Nobz are never above reminding the Boyz who's in charge by making a few bloody examples. This could involve hacking up some suitably impressive foes, or knocking a few fractious Boyz' blocks off. The Nobz aren't too fussy just so long as it gets the message across. Whether clustered in a menacing mob around their Warboss, or lording it over the Boyz, Nobz are a force to be reckoned with. Their armour is usually festooned with kill-trophies, their flesh criss-crossed with impressive scars, earned in pit-fights or while killing their way through strings of brutal wars. Some Nobz even take to the field astride monstrous warbikes, roaring through the enemy ranks like blood-soaked battering rams covered in guns.

	WS	BS	S	T	W	I	A	Ld	Sv	Unit Type	Unit Composition
Nob	4	2	4	4	2	3	3	7	6+	Infantry	2 Nobz
Boss Nob	4	2	4	4	2	3	3	7	6+	Infantry (Character)	1 Boss Nob

WARGEAR:
- **Slugga** (pg 96)
- **Choppa** (pg 93)
- **Stikkbombs** (pg 98)

SPECIAL RULES:
- **'Ere We Go!** (pg 92)
- **Furious Charge**
- **Mob Rule** (pg 92)

OPTIONS:
- May include up to seven additional Nobz.. *18 pts/model*
- Any model may take items from the **Ranged Weapons** and/or **Melee Weapons** lists.
- One Nob may take a Waaagh! banner .... *20 pts*
- Any model may take an ammo runt.. *3 pts/model*
- Any model may take a bosspole.. *5 pts/model*
- The entire mob may take 'eavy armour .... *4 pts/model*
- The entire mob may take warbikes .... *27 pts/model*
- If the unit does not take warbikes, it may select a Trukk (pg 64) or Battlewagon (pg 79) as a Dedicated Transport.

MEGANOBZ

The richest and most battle-hardened Nobz can become Meganobz by paying a Mek to build them a suit of mega armour. Piston-driven and covered in enough protective plating to turn its wearer into a walking tank, this armour is incredibly expensive. Yet it serves as the ultimate greenskin status symbol. Though other Orks mock the Meganobz for wearing so much armour, only the dullest would do so within earshot. Even a direct hit from a tank round is unlikely to do more than knock a Meganob over, worsening his already foul temper. For many, the only chance of surviving an encounter with an angry Meganob is to outrun him. To counteract this weakness, many Meganobz roar into battle aboard armoured wagons. This saves time that would be wasted slogging across the battlefield, and helps the Meganobz get stuck straight in.

	WS	BS	S	T	W	I	A	Ld	Sv	Unit Type	Unit Composition
Meganob	4	2	4	4	2	3	3	7	2+	Infantry	2 Meganobz
Boss Meganob	4	2	4	4	2	3	3	7	2+	Infantry (Character)	1 Boss Meganob

WARGEAR:
- **Twin-linked shoota** (pg 96)
- **Power klaw** (pg 93)
- **Mega armour** (pg 99)
- **Stikkbombs** (pg 98)

SPECIAL RULES:
- **'Ere We Go!** (pg 92)
- **Furious Charge**
- **Mob Rule** (pg 92)

OPTIONS:
- May include up to seven additional Meganobz .... *40 pts/model*
- Any model may replace their twin-linked shoota
  and power klaw with two killsaws .... *10 pts/model*
- Any model may replace their twin-linked shoota with one of the following:
  - Kombi-weapon with rokkit launcha .... *5 pts/model*
  - Kombi-weapon with skorcha .... *5 pts/model*
- Any model may take a bosspole .... *5 pts/model*
- The unit may select a Trukk (pg 70) or Battlewagon (pg 79) as a Dedicated Transport.

KOMMANDOS

Where most Orks love getting stuck in with a minimum of muckin' about, Kommandos prefer to spread panic and fear behind enemy lines. They embody the low cunning common in most Orks, but taken to the extreme. A Kommando would rather sneak up on his victim and stick a dagger through their ribs than just run at them yelling. There can be no greater satisfaction to these Orks than the thump of exploding ammo dumps or the screams of enemies as stikkbombs clatter into their barracks. They especially savour the disbelieving expressions of victims caught in the jaws of a perfect Ork ambush. Festooned with bombs, guns and blades these sneaky gits lurk in the shadows until their boss gives the signal, at which point the Kommandos explode from cover, howling bloody murder and hacking their shocked victims to bits in the name of Gork and Mork.

	WS	BS	S	T	W	I	A	Ld	Sv	Unit Type	Unit Composition
Kommando	4	2	3	4	1	2	2	7	6+	Infantry	5 Kommandos
Boss Nob	4	2	4	4	2	3	3	7	6+	Infantry (Character)	

WARGEAR:
- **Slugga** (pg 96)
- **Choppa** (pg 93)
- **Stikkbombs** (pg 98)

SPECIAL RULES:
- **'Ere We Go!** (pg 92)
- **Furious Charge**
- **Infiltrate**
- **Mob Rule** (pg 92)
- **Move Through Cover**
- **Stealth**

OPTIONS:
- May include up to ten additional Kommandos .... *10 pts/model*
- Up to two Kommandos may replace their sluggas with one of the following:
  - Rokkit launcha .... *5 pts/model*
  - Big shoota .... *5 pts/model*
  - Burna .... *15 pts/model*
- One model may be upgraded to a Boss Nob .... *10 pts*
- The Boss Nob may take items from the **Melee Weapons** lists.
- The Boss Nob may take a bosspole .... *5 pts*

BOSS SNIKROT
THE GREEN GHOST

The infamous Ork Hunters of the Armageddon Imperial Guard are afraid of one Ork and one Ork alone. In the dark nights of the steaming equatorial jungles between Prime and Secundus, these grizzled veterans whisper tales of Boss Snikrot. They tell of a killer who slips through the jungle like a ghost, who can pass through throttlevine groves without disturbing a single leaf. They tell of a savage hunter who lives for slaughter, whose eyes blaze with malice. Finally, they tell of his victims, left to bleed to death with their eyes torn out and their scalps ripped free from their skulls. Snikrot and his Redskull Kommandos have become a bane upon the world of Armageddon, striking from the shadows time and again always where the defenders least expect them. No matter how elaborate Snikrot's schemes become, his ladz are equal to the task, and the Boss has vowed that even if the mighty Ghazghkull has given up on conquering Armageddon, he never will.

	WS	BS	S	T	W	I	A	Ld	Sv	Unit Type	Unit Composition
Boss Snikrot	5	2	5	4	2	3	4	8	6+	Infantry (Character)	1 (Unique)

WARGEAR:
- **Stikkbombs** (pg 98)

SPECIAL RULES:
- **'Ere We Go!** (pg 92)
- **Fear**
- **Furious Charge**
- **Independent Character**
- **Infiltrate**
- **Mob Rule** (pg 92)
- **Move Through Cover**
- **Stealth**

GIFTS OF GORK AND MORK
Mork's Teeth: *These rippy knives are as long as man's arm, and said to be blessed by Mork himself.*

Mork's Teeth are a pair of Melee weapons, each of which has the following profile:

Range	S	AP	Type
-	User	5	Melee, Shred

Ambush: If Boss Snikrot joins a unit of Kommandos that are held in Reserves, and no other Independent Characters join the unit, then Snikrot's unit can move on from any table edge when they arrive from Reserves. No dice roll is required to determine where they enter from; the Ork player chooses. In addition, Boss Snikrot and his unit have their Stealth special rule replaced with the Shrouded special rule on the turn they deploy or arrive from Reserves, until the start of their next turn.

Boss of the Red Skull Kommandos: Boss Snikrot can only join units of Kommandos. If Boss Snikrot is included in a Detachment that includes at least one unit of Kommandos, Boss Snikrot does not take up a slot on the Force Organisation Chart.

TRUKK

Ork Trukks speed into battle at breakneck pace, mobs of Boyz crammed into their rear compartments or hanging recklessly from their hulls. As they close with the foe the Trukks' gunners blaze away wildly. As the enemy lines loom large the driver puts his foot down, squeezing out an extra spurt of acceleration from his ride. With a roar like a predatory beast, the Trukks plough into the enemy's midst before the Boyz on board pile out and get stuck in. Boyz who spend a lot of time fighting and, in some cases, living out of the same Trukk will soon take to personalising their ride with clannish paint jobs, grisly trophies, kill-markings and all manner of dangerous tat. It has been known for entire warbands of Evil Sunz or Freebooterz to form into Trukk mobs, riding to battle in ragged columns amid vast clouds of exhaust-smoke and dust.

		Armour				Unit Type	Unit Composition
	BS	**F**	**S**	**R**	**HP**		
Trukk	2	10	10	10	3	Vehicle (Fast, Open-topped, Transport)	1 Trukk

WARGEAR:
• **Big shoota** (pg 96)

SPECIAL RULES:
Ramshackle: Roll a D6 each time a Trukk suffers a penetrating hit. On the roll of a 6, the Trukk only suffers a glancing hit instead.

TRANSPORT:
Transport Capacity:
Twelve models.

OPTIONS:
• May replace big shoota with rokkit launcha......... *free*
• Trukks may take items from the **Ork Vehicle Equipment** list.

'TRAVELLIN' THROUGH SPACE IS BORING. WELL, BORING UNLESS DA HULK YER ON IS FULL OF DEM GENE-SNEAKERS, OR A BASE FER DA CHAOS LADS WIV DA SPIKES, OR ALREADY HAS BOYZ ON IT. OR IF HUMIE LOOTAS COME CALLIN', THAT'S ALWAYS GOOD FER A BIT A SPORT. OR UNLESS YER HAVE A MUTINY OR TWO TO PASS DA TIME, OR UNLESS STRANGE FINGS START HAPPENIN', WHICH DEY USUALLY DO WHEN YER OUT IN DA WARP. ONE TIME WE HAD SOME BLOODY GREAT UGLY FING COME STRAIGHT OUT OF WEIRD LUGWORT'S 'ED! IT BUTCHERED HALF DA LADS, THAT WAS PRETTY ENTERTAININ'. COME TER FINK OF IT, SPACE IS A PRETTY GOOD LARF. AND THAT'S BEFORE YER FIND YERSELF A NICE NEW WORLD TA CRUSH!'

- Bigmaw, Ork Runtherd

STORMBOYZ

Young and rebellious, Stormboyz strive to stand out amongst the anarchy of Ork society. They studiously ape authority figures, practise things until they can do them right, and openly polish their boots in public places, much to the disgust of their elders. Yet no matter how much they fly in the face of greenskin values with their wilful forward planning and blatant regard for the rules, Stormboyz are still Orks. They live to get stuck into a good, bloody fight as quickly as they can. To this end, Stormboy Korps strike deals with local Meks to equip them with large, noisy rokkit packs. These they use to propel themselves toward the foe amid resounding (and suspiciously well synchronised) bellows of 'Waaagh!', striking the enemy line like ballistic missiles and hacking apart anything unlucky enough to find itself in arm's reach.

	WS	BS	S	T	W	I	A	Ld	Sv	Unit Type	Unit Composition
Stormboy	4	2	3	4	1	2	2	7	6+	Jump Infantry	5 Stormboyz
Boss Nob	4	2	4	4	2	3	3	7	6+	Jump Infantry (Character)	

WARGEAR:
• **Slugga** (pg 96)
• **Choppa** (pg 93)
• **Stikkbombs** (pg 98)
• **Rokkit pack** (pg 98)

SPECIAL RULES:
• **'Ere We Go!** (pg 92)
• **Furious Charge**
• **Mob Rule** (pg 92)

OPTIONS:
• May include up to twenty-five
  additional Stormboyz .... *9 pts/model*
• One model may be upgraded to a Boss Nob .... *10 pts*
• The Boss Nob may take items
  from the **Melee Weapons** list.
• The Boss Nob may take a bosspole .... *5 pts*

DEFFKOPTAS

Deffkoptas buzz across the battlefield, weaving through the sky on a trail of foul-smelling smoke. As they swoop low over the heads of the enemy, the fiendish Ork flying machines fire punishing salvoes of shot, rokkits and bomms into their midst. Leaving flames and blood-splattered craters in their wake, the Deffkoptas jink erratically away, already hunting for their next victims. Deffkoptas are able to navigate over the roughest terrain in order to hunt down the foe. Many get blown out of the sky when first sighted thanks to overconfidence on the part of their warlike pilots. Yet those Orks with a real knack for the job have the self-control to locate the enemy then lead the rest of the Boyz down on top of them. These rare greenskins take pride in finding the best scraps for the rest of the tribe to get stuck into, before diving down to join the fun.

	WS	BS	S	T	W	I	A	Ld	Sv	Unit Type	Unit Composition
Deffkopta	4	2	3	5	2	2	2	7	4+	Jetbike	1 Deffkopta

WARGEAR:
- **Twin-linked big shoota** (pg 96)
- **Choppa** (pg 93)

SPECIAL RULES:
- **'Ere We Go!** (pg 92)
- **Furious Charge**
- **Hit & Run**
- **Mob Rule** (pg 92)
- **Scout**

OPTIONS:
- May include up to four additional Deffkoptas .... *30 pts/model*
- Any Deffkopta may replace their twin-linked big shoota with one of the following:
  - Twin-linked rokkit launcha ....*free*
  - Kustom mega-blasta ....*free*
- Any Deffkopta may be equipped with:
  - Bigbomm .... *15 pts/model*
  - Buzzsaw .... *25 pts/model*

DAKKAJET

Streaking into battle through war-scorched skies, a Dakkajet's massive thruster leaves an oily contrail of black smoke in its wake even as its guns spit streams of bullets at the foe. Though not as nimble as the aircraft of some other races, Dakkajets are capable of an incredible turn of speed that makes them a fearsome enemy to face in aerial combat. It also helps that Orks fly like complete headcases. Dakkajet pilots are great believers in quantity over quality. As such they ensure the Meks strap every gun available to the fuselages of their 'jet. In the heat of battle, while corkscrewing madly through formations of enemy aircraft, Dakkajet pilots will cut loose with an absolute storm of fire. Some have even been known to smash out their cockpit glass with the butts of their sluggas in order to add their own pistol-fire to that of their plane. All of this makes Dakkajet pilots unusually effective shots; with so many bullets fired, some are bound to hit the target.

	BS	F	S	R	HP	Unit Type	Unit Composition
Dakkajet	2	10	10	10	3	Vehicle (Flyer)	1 Dakkajet

(Armour: F S R)

WARGEAR:
- **Two twin-linked supa shootas** (pg 96)

SPECIAL RULES:
- **Strafing Run**
- **Supersonic**
- **Waaagh! Plane**

OPTIONS:
- May take a red paint job.................................... *5 pts*
- May take an additional twin-linked supa shoota............. *20 pts*
- May take a flyboss .... *15 pts*

Waaagh! Plane: During a turn in which a Waaagh! is called, each of this model's Assault weapons fires one more shot than normal.

THE DEFF SKWADRON
Led by Flyboss Kommanda Uzgob, the Deff Skwadron were one of the most infamous formations of Ork flyboys in recent memory. Surviving dozens of sorties in the bloody war between Warbosses Badthug and Grimlug, Uzgob's airborne loons were responsible for the deployment of the 'Gantbuster bomb in Scrap Alley, the sinking of Grimlug's battleship, and the aerial deployment of over five thousand angry squigs into Warboss Grimlug's main encampment. Screaming into battle with all guns blazing, the Deff Skwadron were known for 'gettin' their retribution in first'.

BURNA-BOMMER

Burna-bommers are an inevitable by-product of the Orks' love for speed, fire, and the desire to combine these things while killing something. Strapped with as many incendiary bombs and rockets as is physically feasible, Burna-bommers streak low over the battlefield, raining conflagrant death down on tightly-packed enemy infantry. The wild-eyed Burna Boy pilots of these craft like to watch their targets burn 'up close and crispy'. As such they regularly return to base with their undercarriage streaked with gore and scorch marks. Burna-bommers sometimes carry skorcha missiles, making them even more deadly. These corkscrewing missiles make a mockery of fortifications, their warheads bursting in conflagatory showers that drive their victims from cover, or else cook them alive within defences turned death-traps.

		Armour				Unit Type	Unit Composition
	BS	F	S	R	HP		
Burna-bommer	2	10	10	10	3	Vehicle (Flyer)	1 Burna-bommer

WARGEAR:
- **Twin-linked big shoota** (pg 96)
- **Twin-linked supa shoota** (pg 96)
- **Two burna bombs** (pg 94)

SPECIAL RULES:
- **Supersonic**
- **Waaagh! Plane** (pg 73)

OPTIONS:
- May take up to six skorcha missiles .... *10 pts each*
- May take a red paint job .... *5 pts*

Grot Gunner: When a model with this special rule fires a big shoota or twin-linked big shoota, these shots are resolved at Ballistic Skill 3.

BLITZA-BOMMER

Even on their best day, the average Ork flyboy has little patience for trajectories, payload arcs, and all the other 'boring bits' of high-altitude bombing. Blitza-bommer pilots instead ensure their massively unsubtle boom bombs land more-or-less on target by simply dropping them from point-blank range. To pull this off, Blitza-bommer pilots throw their craft into screaming nose-dives, their terrified grot bombardiers pulling the bomm-release lever at the last possible moment. After a loud clank and some alarming juddering, the bomb plunges groundward and explodes more-or-less on target with a thunderous bang. With his payload away, the cackling flyboy (hopefully) pulls up. These manoeuvres don't always end well, and most grots have to be forcibly nailed into their bombardier's nests to avoid them bailing out before take-off.

	BS	F	S	R	HP	Unit Type	Unit Composition
		┌ Armour ┐					
Blitza-bommer	2	10	10	10	3	Vehicle (Flyer)	1 Blitza-bommer

WARGEAR:
- **Big shoota** (pg 96)
- **Twin-linked supa shoota** (pg 96)
- **Two boom bombs** (pg 94)

SPECIAL RULES:
- **Grot Gunner** (see opposite)
- **Supersonic**
- **Waaagh! Plane** (pg 73)

OPTIONS:
- May take a red paint job.......................................*5 pts*

WARBIKERS

Mobs of Ork Warbikers race into battle at suicidal speeds, exhausts belching greasy clouds of smoke. As they hurtle toward the enemy ranks, the Warbikers fill the air with a murderous storm of shots from their blazing dakkaguns. Surrounded by billowing clouds of smoke and dust, the Warbikers are protected from the worst of the enemy's return fire – by the time the bikeboyz thunder out of this swirling cloud, they are all but on top of the foe. Wide-eyed and panting behind goggles and dust-masks, most Warbikers' need for speed is such that they can barely stand to stay still for five minutes. The more canny Warbosses use this to their advantage, sending their Warbikers to trigger traps and ambushes prematurely, to run down enemy supply convoys, or to soften up the foes' defences before the rest of the tribe gives them a good stomping.

	WS	BS	S	T	W	I	A	Ld	Sv	Unit Type	Unit Composition
Warbiker	4	2	3	5	1	2	2	7	4+	Bike	3 Warbikers
Boss Nob	4	2	4	5	2	3	3	7	4+	Bike (Character)	

WARGEAR:
- **Slugga** (pg 96)
- **Choppa** (pg 93)
- **Warbike** (pg 98)

SPECIAL RULES:
- **'Ere We Go!** (pg 92)
- **Furious Charge**
- **Mob Rule** (pg 92)

OPTIONS:
- May include up to twelve additional Warbikers .... *18 pts/model*
- One model may be upgraded to a Boss Nob .... *10 pts*
- The Boss Nob may take items from the **Melee Weapons** lists.
- The Boss Nob may take a bosspole..................................... *5 pts*

WAZDAKKA GUTZMEK
Wazdakka Gutzmek, creator of the fabled Bike of the Aporkalypse, is the greatest Ork bikeboy of them all. After being accused of cheating when he won the Race of the Burning Wheels, Wazdakka levelled his tribe's settlement with his dakkacannons and roared off in disgust. From that day forth he has roamed the stars, a deadly bike-boss for hire. Lately Wazdakka's wanderings have taken on overtones of a holy pilgrimage, Speed Freeks flocking to his banner with every victory. Gutzmek himself claims that he will lead his smoke-belching and unstoppable Waaagh! from one end of space to the other, the greatest race in the history of time and one that is sure to please Gork and Mork immensely.

WARBUGGIES

Orks tend toward light, fast vehicles with big guns that can be cobbled together from any junk to hand. Most are crewed by a mad-eyed Ork driver and cackling gunner, with perhaps a grot or two hanging on for dear life. What they lack in survivability, these crude vehicles make up for in speed, numbers and dakka. They encircle the enemy in speeding squadrons, guns blazing wildly while their crew throw their heads back and howl like Madboyz. Most consist of little more than chassis, engine, gubbins and a sizeable gun, and are capable of an impressive turn of speed. For traversing dense terrain, some Warbuggies will be converted into the half-track Wartrakks, while the addition of a jutting flamethrower, some sloshing fuel tanks and a crew of slavering Burna Boyz transforms a Warbuggy into the much feared Skorcha.

		Armour				Unit Type	Unit Composition
	BS	F	S	R	HP		
Warbuggy	2	10	10	10	2	Vehicle (Fast, Open-topped)	1 Warbuggy
Skorcha	2	10	10	10	2	Vehicle (Fast, Open-topped)	
Wartrakk	2	10	10	10	2	Vehicle (Fast, Open-topped)	

WARGEAR:

Warbuggy:
- Twin-linked
  big shoota (pg 96)

Skorcha:
- Skorcha (pg 94)

Wartrakk:
- Twin-linked
  big shoota (pg 96)

SPECIAL RULES:
- Outflank

Trakked: (Skorcha and Wartrakk only) The vehicle re-rolls failed Dangerous Terrain tests.

OPTIONS:
- May include up to four additional Warbuggies .... *25 pts/model*
- Any Warbuggy may be upgraded to a Wartrakk ...... *5 pts/model*
- Any Warbuggy may be upgraded to a Skorcha ..... *10 pts/model*
- Any Warbuggy or Wartrakk may replace its twin-linked big
  shoota with a twin-linked rokkit launcha .... *free*
- Any model take any of the following:
  - Red paint job .... *5 pts/model*
  - Extra armour .... *10 pts/model*
  - Grot riggers.. *10 pts/model*

MEK GUNZ

18 POINTS

The roar of Mek Gunz has heralded the end for many a hapless foe. Spitting out blasts of crackling energy, swatting planes out of the air or crushing their victims in crackling fists of bright green force, these big, clanky field guns have enough dakka to stomp even the toughest targets. Of course, as no self-respecting Ork would be left behind when there's a fight in the offing, crewing the gunz is left to the long-suffering grots. The Orks drag the Mek Gunz into battle behind speeding wagons and Trukks before abandoning them in a heap and leaving the grots to sort them out. Though capable of blasting a tank in half or scything down enemy infantry, these weapons are just as likely to backfire explosively. The biggest hazard for enemies facing Mek Gunz is that, until they start firing, no-one is really sure what they will do.

	WS	BS	S	T	W	I	A	Ld	Sv	Unit Type	Unit Composition
Mek Gun	-	-	-	7	2	-	-	-	3+	Artillery	1 Mek Gun
Gretchin	2	3	2	2	1	2	1	5	-	Artillery	2 Gretchin

WARGEAR:

Gretchin:
- **Close combat weapon**

Mek Gun:
- **Kannon** (pg 95)

OPTIONS:
- May include up to four additional Mek Gunz (each including two Gretchin) .... *18 pts/model*
- Each Mek Gun can include up to two additional Gretchin.. *3 pts/model*
- Each Mek Gun can include one ammo runt .... *3 pts/model*
- Any Mek Gun can replace its kannon with one of the following:
  - Lobba ....*free*
  - Zzap gun .... *5 pts/model*
  - Bubblechukka... *12 pts/model*
  - Kustom mega-kannon .... *12 pts/model*
  - Smasha gun.. *12 pts/model*
  - Traktor kannon .... *12 pts/model*

BATTLEWAGON

Ork Battlewagons rumble to war on a collection of tracks, tyres and massive spiked rollers. Whether lumbering gun-fortresses, bright red speedsters or gaudy rust buckets smeared with Ork glyphs, Battlewagons are massive slabs of motorised junk built to carry big mobs of greenskins into battle. No matter each Battlewagon's individual peculiarities, all fulfil the essential role of armoured attack vehicle. A solid wedge of these mighty tanks can provide a warband with a (somewhat rusty) mailed fist that can be jammed right down the throat of the enemy army. With guns booming and deff rollas coated in mud and gore, Ork Battlewagons carve a path of bloody ruin through the foe while their Ork passengers blaze away at the dazed survivors, and bellow "Waaagh!" at the top of their lungs.

	BS	F	S	R	HP	Unit Type	Unit Composition
		Armour					
Battlewagon	2	14	12	10	4	Vehicle (Tank, Open-topped, Transport)	1 Battlewagon

WARGEAR:
• None

TRANSPORT:
Transport Capacity: Twenty models. If the Battlewagon mounts a killkannon it may only carry twelve models.

Fire Points: If a Battlewagon has the 'ard case upgrade it has five Fire Points, two on either side of the hull and one at the rear.

Access Points: If a Battlewagon has the 'ard case upgrade it has three Access Points, one on either side of the hull and one at the rear.

OPTIONS:
• May take a killkannon .... *30 pts*
• May take one of the following weapons:
 - Kannon .... *10 pts*
 - Lobba .... *10 pts*
 - Zzap gun .... *10 pts*
• May take up to four of the following weapons
 in any combination:
 - Big shoota .... *5 pts each*
 - Rokkit launcha .... *5 pts each*
• May take any of the following:
 - Deff rolla .... *10 pts*
 - 'Ard case .... *15 pts*
 - Grabbin' klaw .... *5 pts*
• Battlewagons may take items from the **Ork Vehicle Equipment** list.

DEFF DREAD

Deff Dreads are clanking monstrosities that behave in battle much like enormous metal Orks. They clank toward the foe, waving piston-driven arms that end in saws, claws and really big guns. Lurching along as fast as their hydraulic legs will carry them, their bellows of 'Waaagh!' echo from in-built speakers at earsplitting volume. Though all this is hugely entertaining for Orks fighting alongside a Deff Dread, for enemies it is utterly terrifying. Deff Dreads epitomise the unstoppable ferocity of the greenskin race, and the damage they can do is jaw-dropping. The brutal implantation surgery and subsequent claustrophobia tends to drive Deff Dread pilots a bit bonkers. They will take any opportunity to vent their frustrations violently upon the foe, if only to make themselves feel better about having to eat everything through a straw...

	WS	BS	S	F	S	R	I	A	HP	Unit Type	Unit Composition
					Armour						
Deff Dread	4	2	5	12	12	10	2	3	3	Vehicle (Walker)	1 Deff Dread

WARGEAR:
- **Two big shootas** (pg 96)
- **Two power klaws** (pg 93)

OPTIONS:
- May replace any of its big shootas with one of the following:
  - Rokkit launcha ....*free*
  - Kustom mega-blasta ....*5 pts*
  - Skorcha ....*5 pts*
  - Power klaw ....*10 pts*
- May take any of the following:
  - Grot riggers..*10 pts*
  - Extra armour ....*10 pts*

KILLA KANS

Killa Kans bear many similarities to Deff Dreads, with their snipping klawz, chugging heavy weapons, and lumpy metal hulls. Yet in place of an enraged Ork, Killa Kans are piloted by cackling grots. Though individually smaller than a Deff Dread, Killa Kans charge toward the enemy lines in jostling mobs of riveted iron and roaring saw-blades. The Killa Kans' grot pilots put their relative skill with firearms to good use, blowing the zog out of anything unlucky enough to cross their path. Despite being hardwired into a ten-foot tall killing machine, Killa Kan pilots still retain a good degree of Gretchin cowardice. As a result they still believe in safety in numbers, and have a bad habit of losing their nerve under fire. It is not unheard of for Killa Kans to waddle about in circles or freeze up entirely at the first sign of danger.

	WS	BS	S	F	S	R	I	A	HP	Unit Type	Unit Composition
Killa Kan	2	3	5	11	11	10	2	2	2	Vehicle (Walker)	1 Killa Kan

Armour column spans F, S, R.

WARGEAR:
- **Big shoota** (pg 96)
- **Kan klaw** (pg 93)

SPECIAL RULES:

Cowardly Grots!: If a unit of Killa Kans suffers 25% or more casualties during any one phase, the unit must roll a D6 at the end of that phase. Add +1 to the dice roll if there are three or more Killa Kans in the unit, and a further +1 if there are one or more Deff Dreads within 6" of the unit. On a result of 3+ the test is passed and nothing happens. On a result of 1-2 the test is failed and every model in the unit immediately suffers a Crew Shaken result. Note that no models lose a Hull Point as a result of a failed Cowardly Grots! test.

OPTIONS:
- May include up to five additional Killa Kans .... *50 pts/model*
- Any Killa Kan can replace their big shoota with one of the following:
  - Rokkit launcha .... *free*
  - Grotzooka .... *5 pts/model*
  - Kustom mega-blasta .... *5 pts/model*
  - Skorcha .... *5 pts/model*
- Any Killa Kan can take any of the following:
  - Grot riggers .... *5 pts/model*
  - Extra armour .... *10 pts/model*

GORKANAUT

245 POINTS

A Gorkanaut is everything an Ork aspires to be. Massive, tough, loud and destructive, its blocky silhouette looms menacingly over friend and foe alike. From its hulking, orkoid shape to the brutal weapons it wields, a Gorkanaut epitomises the unsubtle brutality of Gork and his no-nonsense way of war. Every Gorkanaut is essentially a massively overbuilt armoured war suit bristling with dakka and packing an armoured claw the size of a Killa Kan. They are ideal for a lone Nob who wants to make a name for himself, serving as weapon, transport and (rather cramped and smelly) home all in one. Gorkanauts have become especially popular in recent years as more greenskins are seized by visions of the Great Waaagh! and find themselves compelled to pilot these mighty engines into battle, trampling their panicked foes as they go.

				Armour							
	WS	BS	S	F	S	R	I	A	HP	Unit Type	Unit Composition
Gorkanaut	4	2	8	13	13	12	2	4	5	Vehicle (Walker, Transport)	1 Gorkanaut

WARGEAR:
- **Deffstorm mega-shoota** (pg 96)
- **Two twin-linked big shootas** (pg 96)
- **Two rokkit launchas** (pg 95)
- **Skorcha**
- **Klaw of Gork (or possibly Mork)** (pg 93)

SPECIAL RULES:
- **Rampage**

TRANSPORT:
Transport Capacity: Six models.
Fire Points: None.
Access Points: A Gorkanaut has one Access Point at the front.

OPTIONS:
- May take any of the following:
  - Extra armour .... *10 pts*
  - Grot riggers... *20 pts*

MORKANAUT

Where Gorkanauts epitomise the unsubtle brutality of almighty Gork, a Morkanaut displays all the lethal kunnin' of equally almighty Mork. Every Morkanaut is personally built and piloted by a skilled Mekboy, and packs a wild array of energy weapons and glowy gubbinz from the Mek's own workshop. Morkanaut pilots – like their Gorkanaut equivalents – are usually outcasts. Some feel the call of the Great Waaagh! and set out to cause carnage in the name of Mork, while others hunt like (violent) magpies for the technological secrets of other races. A rare few, known as Badmeks, will be ejected forcibly from their tribe for crimes such as using the local Weirdboy tower for target practise. These rogue pilots are especially dangerous, and will often begin their wanderings by flattening their former tribe's settlement with their Morkanaut's guns.

	WS	BS	S	F	S	R	I	A	HP	Unit Type	Unit Composition
				┌─Armour─┐							
Morkanaut	4	2	8	13	13	12	2	4	5	Vehicle (Walker, Transport)	1 Morkanaut

WARGEAR:
- **Two twin-linked big shootas** (pg 96)
- **Kustom mega-blasta** (pg 95)
- **Kustom mega-kannon** (pg 95)
- **Two rokkit launchas** (pg 95)
- **Klaw of Gork (or possibly Mork)** (pg 93)

TRANSPORT:
Transport Capacity: Six models.
Fire Points: None.
Access Points: A Morkanaut has one Access Point at the front.

OPTIONS:
- May take a kustom force field .... *50 pts*
- May take any of the following:
  - Extra armour .... *10 pts*
  - Grot riggers .... *20 pts*

LOOTAS

Toting massive deffguns that fill the air with a rain of shots, rokkits and energy blasts, Loota mobs provide a warband with much needed and extremely heavy covering fire. When a mob of Lootas cuts loose, the overwhelming storm of dakka they create churns infantry to a blood-soaked pulp while tanks shudder and clang, their crews and systems perforated until the vehicles shudder to a halt leaking oil and gore. Lootas tend to be about the heaviest armed Orks going, largely due to their natural flair for larceny, cons and general light-fingered thievery. They often befriend Meks, trading their ill-gotten gains for ever more kustom dakka. Many Mekboys cannot resist tinkering with the deffguns' worky bits even as the Lootas begin firing, preventing messy mishaps and ensuring that they perform to their full, devastating potential.

	WS	BS	S	T	W	I	A	Ld	Sv	Unit Type	Unit Composition
Loota	4	2	3	4	1	2	2	7	6+	Infantry	5 Lootas
Mek	4	2	3	4	1	2	2	7	6+	Infantry (Character)	

WARGEAR:
- **Deffgun** (pg 95)
- **Stikkbombs** (pg 98)

SPECIAL RULES:
- **'Ere We Go!** (pg 92)
- **Furious Charge**
- **Mob Rule** (pg 92)

OPTIONS:
- May include up to ten additional Lootas .... *14 pts/model*
- Up to three models may be upgraded to Meks, replacing their deffgun with Mek's tools, slugga and choppa.. *free*
- Any Mek may be accompanied by a grot oiler... *5 pts/model*
- Any Mek may replace his choppa with a killsaw .... *20 pts/model*
- Any Mek may take items from the **Mek Weapons** list.
- The unit may select a Trukk as a Dedicated Transport (pg 70).

FLASH GITZ

The gun-crazy showoffs known as Flash Gitz are skilled at breaking heads up close or blasting their enemies into tiny, glowing bits with equal style. Amongst the richest and most obnoxious of their warlike breed, Flash Gitz travel the galaxy engaging in acts of outrageous piracy and wanton vandalism. They hire themselves out as mercenaries to Ork warbands, basking in the envy of Boyz jealous of their flashy kit and prodigious dakka. Despite their ostentation, Flash Gitz give a Warboss all the killpower he pays for. Completely lethal in gun battles, boarding actions and the like, a mob of Gitz opening fire is nothing short of cataclysmic. A punishing hail of energy bolts and bullets fills the air, the Flash Gitz' victims coming apart amid sprays of blood and blossoms of flame before the Gitz stomp the life out of anyone left standing.

	WS	BS	S	T	W	I	A	Ld	Sv	Unit Type	Unit Composition
Flash Git	4	2	4	4	2	3	3	7	6+	Infantry	4 Flash Gitz
Kaptin	4	2	4	4	2	3	3	7	6+	Infantry (Character)	1 Kaptin

WARGEAR:
- **Snazzgun** (pg 96)
- **Stikkbombs** (pg 98)
- **Bosspole** (pg 98)
- **Gitfinda** (pg 98)

SPECIAL RULES:
- **'Ere We Go!** (pg 92)
- **Furious Charge**
- **Mob Rule** (pg 92)

OPTIONS:
- May include up to five additional Flash Gitz .... *22 pts/model*
- Any model may take an ammo runt .... *3 pts/model*
- The unit may select a Trukk (pg 70) or Battlewagon (pg 79) as a Dedicated Transport.

'THE ORKS PLAGUE THE GALAXY FROM END TO END WITH THEIR CEASELESS WARRING AND STRIFE. THEY ARE A RACE SO DEEPLY ROOTED IN WAR THAT PEACE IS UTTERLY INCOMPREHENSIBLE TO THEM. THEY CANNOT BE BARGAINED WITH OR BOUGHT SAVE WITH WEAPONS THAT THEY WILL INEVITABLY TURN AGAINST THOSE WHO TRIED TO BRIBE THEM. I PRAY WITH ALL MY FAITH THAT SOME GREAT CATASTROPHE WILL ANNIHILATE THEM BUT I FEAR THAT ULTIMATELY IT IS THEY, NOT WE, WHO SHALL RULE THE GALAXY'.

- Xanthius, High Lord of Terra

GHAZGHKULL THRAKA

THE BEAST OF ARMAGEDDON

Ghazghkull Mag Uruk Thraka is a mighty prophet of the Waaagh!. He is the single most influential Ork in the galaxy, and billions of greenskins march to war in his name. Since Ghazghkull's rise to power, he has led countless campaigns of destruction. He has crushed Eldar war hosts, banished tides of Daemons, and smashed phalanxes of Necrons to so much sparking scrap. Yet his greatest battles have always been fought against the servants of the Emperor. Ghazghkull's sheer, unstoppable brutality has left countless worlds of the Imperium blazing in his wake and reduced mighty Armageddon to a never-ending cauldron of war. Yet Ghazghkull is not satisfied. Gork and Mork have greater plans for their prophet, plans they see fit to deliver amid agonising visions of a galaxy ablaze with green fire. At their behest, Ghazghkull is beginning his greatest work. He will travel the galaxy, subjugating every Warlord and gathering every Ork to his banner until the stars themselves shudder to the thundering footfalls of his horde. Ghazghkull is gathering the Waaagh! of Gork and Mork themselves, a Waaagh! that will drown the galaxy in a war so great that the gods themselves will tear their way out of the Warp to join the fight.

	WS	BS	S	T	W	I	A	Ld	Sv	Unit Type	Unit Composition
Ghazghkull Thraka	6	2	5	5	4	4	5	9	2+	Infantry (Character)	1 (Unique)

WARGEAR:
- Cybork body (pg 98)
- Mega armour (pg 99)
- Big shoota (pg 96)
- Power klaw (pg 93)
- Bosspole (pg 98)
- Stikkbombs (pg 98)

WARLORD TRAIT:
- Prophet of the Waaagh!
  (pg 92)

SPECIAL RULES:
- 'Ere We Go! (pg 92)
- Eternal Warrior
- Furious Charge
- Independent Character
- Mob Rule (pg 92)
- Waaagh! (pg 54)

Prophet of Gork and Mork: If Ghazghkull is your Warlord, he gains a 2+ Invulnerable save on any turn he calls a Waaagh! This invulnerable save lasts until the start of his next turn. In addition, Ghazghkull and all other models in his unit that are equipped with mega armour can Run on a turn he calls a Waaagh! despite having the Slow and Purposeful special rule (which is conferred by wearing mega armour).

OPTIONS:
- Ghazghkull Thraka may take items from the **Runts & Squigs** list.

A Stompa is an effigy of war built by the Orks to ape their brutal gods. Cobbled together in typical Ork fashion, the Stompa's bulk is festooned with overlapping metal plates, bolted atop one another to present a formidable frame and allow the Stompa to shrug off incoming firepower. It has a large crew of Orks and grots to keep its vast engine going and its weapons blazing away. And Stompas are festooned with weapons – ranging from big shootas and skorchas poking out from between their protective plates to the deff kannon, an enormous piece of ordnance, and the bullet-spewing supa-gatler. A Stompa can also carry a full mob of Orks to war, ready to jump out and put the boot in at a moment's notice. Once in combat, a Stompa wields its mega-choppa – a massive whirring blade that can cleave a bastion in two or hack a Titan down to size in a flurry of roaring violence.

	WS	BS	S	Armour F	Armour S	Armour R	I	A	HP	Unit Type	Unit Composition
Stompa	4	2	10	13	13	12	1	4	12	Vehicle (Super-heavy Walker, Transport)	1 Stompa

WARGEAR:
- **Three big shootas** (pg 96)
- **Deff kannon** (pg 95)
- **Skorcha** (pg 94)
- **Supa-gatler** (pg 96)
- **Three supa-rokkits** (pg 97)
- **Twin-linked big shoota** (pg 96)
- **Mega-choppa** (pg 93)

SPECIAL RULES:
Effigy: All friendly units with the Orks Faction that are within 6" of a Stompa have the Fearless special rule.

TRANSPORT:
Transport Capacity: Twenty models.
Fire Points: Four; three in its belly, one in its head.
Access Points: A Stompa has one Access Point at the rear.

OPTIONS:
- May take up to two additional supa-rokkits ....*20 pts each*
- May take grot riggers..*30 pts*

ORK WARBAND

Ork warbands infest the galaxy from end to end, and they vary greatly in size and composition. Wherever they come from, they will inevitably include the Warboss that united them in the first place, a hard core of his most dangerous warriors, and a teeming mass of Boyz drawn to the promise of carnage. Orks draw great strength from their numbers, the Waaagh! energy that courses through each greenskin amplified by the bellowing mass of battle-hungry maniacs charging towards the enemy lines. This mysterious force can be harnessed by a canny Warboss to drive his ladz into a killing frenzy at a critical moment, driving them forward in a ground-pounding stampede that can overrun the most stubborn of enemy gunlines. Even the Gretchin brave enough to accompany the Boyz try to make themselves heard over the deafening volume of the Ork battlecry; they give it their best shot, biting and scrabbling at the enemy's weak spots in their eagerness for the kill. Needless to say the true danger comes from the charging Orks themselves, a thunderous mass of muscle, metal and bad attitude that slams headlong into the foe before breaking apart to hack and slay with joyous abandon.

FORMATION:

- 1 Warboss (pg 54)
- 1 Mek (pg 56)
- 1 unit of Nobz (pg 66) or Meganobz (pg 67)
- 6 units of Boyz (pg 62)
- 1 unit of Gretchin (pg 63)

RESTRICTIONS:
None.

COMMAND BENEFITS:

Boss of Da Waaagh!: If this Detachment is chosen as your Primary Detachment, you can re-roll the result when rolling on the Warlord Traits table in *Codex: Orks*.

The Greenskin Hordes: Every unit with 10 or more models in this Detachment gains the Hammer of Wrath special rule in any Assault phase in which it successfully charges an enemy unit and the dice rolled for its charge range is 10 or more (before modifiers). Note that the unit does not need to move the full distance rolled to gain this effect and it does not matter if the unit's size is reduced below 10 models during its charge (as a result of Overwatch, Dangerous Terrain tests etc.) so long as it can still successfully make the charge.

Stampede: If the formation's Warboss is your Warlord he can use his Waaagh! special rule each and every turn after the first.

APPENDIX

This section of the book details many of the rules for using an Ork army in your games of Warhammer 40,000, including their unique special rules, Warlord Traits, wargear and psychic powers, Tactical Objectives and the Ork Horde detachment. The reference section at the end summarises the rules from throughout this codex, and provides unit and weapons profiles.

ORK SPECIAL RULES

An Ork army uses a number of special rules that are common to several of its units. These are collected and explained here, in full, for your convenience. Special rules that are unique to particular units are presented in the relevant entry instead. Other, more common, rules are simply listed by name – these are described in full in the Special Rules section of *Warhammer 40,000: The Rules*.

'ERE WE GO!
Ever eager to get stuck into the fray, Orks will barrel across the battlefield as quick as they can when the foe is in their sights.

If every model in a unit has this special rule, the unit can re-roll a single dice when determining its charge range.

MOB RULE
Orks are simplistic, brutal creatures who love to fight and draw confidence from possessing strength in numbers.

If every model in a unit has this special rule, and the unit fails a Morale check or Pinning test (after any re-rolls they may have), roll immediately on the following table:

D6	RESULT
1	**Born to Fight:** *Orks love fighting, and the prospect of a good punch-up will sometimes stop them from running off.* If the unit is locked in combat, it is treated as if it had passed the Morale check or Pinning test. If the unit is not locked in combat, it fails the Morale check or Pinning test.
2-3	**Breaking Heads:** *The mob's leader knocks a few heads together until the ladz settle down and get back in the fight.* If the unit includes one or more Ork characters (including Independent Characters), it suffers D6 Strength 4 AP- hits, and is then treated as if it had passed the Morale check or Pinning test. These hits are Randomly Allocated, but cannot be allocated to Ork characters (any excess hits are lost). If the unit does not include any Ork characters, it fails the Morale check or Pinning test.
4-6	**Squabble:** *A brawl breaks out as the Orks decide what to do. When the dust settles, nobody can remember what the trouble was about in the first place.* If the unit has 10 or more models, it suffers D6 Strength 4 AP- hits, and is then treated as if it had passed the Morale check or Pinning test. The hits are Randomly Allocated. If the unit has fewer than 10 models, it fails the Morale check or Pinning test.

WARLORD TRAITS

When generating its Warlord Trait, an Ork Warlord can either roll on one of the Warlord Traits tables in *Warhammer 40,000: The Rules*, or roll on the table below.

WARLORD TRAITS TABLE

D6	WARLORD TRAIT
1	**Prophet of the Waaagh!:** *Mork (or possibly Gork) has chosen this Warlord for greatness, and every Ork under his command knows it.* The Warlord gains the Waaagh! special rule (pg 54). If the Warlord already has the Waaagh! special rule then, in addition to the usual effects, all friendly models with the 'Ere We Go! special rule gain the Fearless special rule when he calls a Waaagh!, until the start of their next turn.
2	**Bellowing Tyrant:** *This Warlord is an unholy terror, a roaring lunatic whose every (very loud) word is law.* The Warlord, and all friendly units with the Orks Faction within 12" of him, re-roll failed Morale checks and Pinning tests.
3	**Like a Thunderbolt!:** *This Warlord is a master of the all-out, no-holds-barred, headlong charge into battle.* The Warlord, and all friendly units with the Orks Faction within 12" of him, can re-roll all the dice when determining Run moves or charge range.
4	**Brutal but Kunnin':** *This Warlord has a sneaky streak a mile wide and knows just where to hit his foes.* The Warlord can re-roll one failed To Hit or To Wound roll each turn.
5	**Kunnin' but Brutal:** *The Warlord knows when to roll with a punch, and can shrug off the hardest blows.* The Warlord can re-roll one failed armour or invulnerable saving throw each turn.
6	**Might is Right:** *Made of muscle and aggression, this Warlord is the embodiment of the Orks' warlike nature.* The Warlord receives +1 to the Strength characteristic on his profile.

GUBBINZ AND GUNZ

This section of *Codex: Orks* lists all the weapons and equipment used by the Orks, along with rules for using them in your games of Warhammer 40,000. Equipment that is carried by named characters is detailed in the appropriate entry in the datasheets (pg 54-89), while weapons and equipment used by all other types of units are detailed here.

MELEE WEAPONS

> Profiles for the weapons in this section are also listed in the reference section (pg 104). The full rules for the following melee weapon can be found in *Warhammer 40,000: The Rules*:
>
> Close combat weapon

BUZZSAW

Simple articulated arms mounting industrial chainsaw attachments, buzzsaws allow Deffkopta pilots to perform 'fly-by decapitations' on luckless victims below.

Range	S	AP	Type
-	x2	2	Melee, Unwieldy, Specialist Weapon

CHOPPA WEAPONS

Orks use a variety of bladed weapons and chain-blades. The largest hand-held choppas can bisect most foes in a single swing, whilst those mounted on Stompas can slice a Titan in two.

	Range	S	AP	Type
Choppa	-	User	-	Melee
Big choppa	-	+2	5	Melee, Two-handed
Mega-choppa	-	D	1	Melee

GRABBA STIKK

This is the traditional tool of the Runtherd, used for throttling anything in arm's reach with its rusty, spring-loaded spikes.

Range	S	AP	Type
-	User	-	Melee, Throttle

Throttle: When the wielder is fighting in a challenge, his opponent reduces their Attacks characteristic by 1 (to a minimum of 1).

GROT-PROD

This simple Mekboy invention delivers a short, sharp shock to an errant grot's squishy bits. The voltage of these weapons can be cranked up considerably, allowing their wielder to really get stuck in.

Range	S	AP	Type
-	User	-	Melee, High Voltage

High Voltage: When the wielder makes its close combat Attacks, it can instead choose to make a single High Voltage Attack. If it does so, roll To Hit as normal, but resolve the Attack at double the wielder's Strength (to a maximum of 10) for the purposes of that Attack.

KILLSAW

These massive, roaring bladesaws can carve a tank in two, or saw foes into bloody, ripped-up ruin.

Range	S	AP	Type
-	x2	2	Melee, Armourbane, Specialist Weapon, Unwieldy

KLAW WEAPONS

Orks favour brutal power klaws over the more sophisticated power fists of other races. These huge hydraulic shears are capable of rending and crushing even the toughest foes. Ork walkers are fitted with klaws that befit their greater size, and can rip through anything foolish enough to stand in the pilot's way.

	Range	S	AP	Type
Power klaw	-	x2	2	Melee, Unwieldy, Specialist Weapon
Kan klaw	-	+2	2	Melee
Klaw of Gork (or possibly Mork)	-	10	1	Melee, Concussive

TANKHAMMER

The tankhammer is, in truth, a rocket on a stick. This explosive maul is swung with homicidal enthusiasm into the most vulnerable parts of the victim, be it a tank or a luckless enemy warrior.

Range	S	AP	Type
-	8	3	Melee, Two-handed, Unwieldy

'URTY SYRINGE

The congealed sludge that Painboyz inject as a clotting agent has fatal effects upon non-orkoid physiology. Arteries clog with fungal growth, lungs become spore-bloated puffballs, and the victim quickly collapses with porridgey froth bubbling from every orifice.

Range	S	AP	Type
-	User	-	Melee, Poisoned (4+)

WEIRDBOY STAFF

The shiny charms and jangling bells that bedeck a Weirdboy staff belie the horrific damage they can wreak in battle. The copper pole at their core allows their wielder to earth the rampant Waaagh! energy that riddles them, and these weapons discharge crackling green blasts with every blow the Weirdboy lands.

Range	S	AP	Type
-	+2	4	Melee, Force, Two-handed

RANGED WEAPONS

BIGBOMM

Some Deffkopta pilots will strap big explosive shells beneath their chugging steeds.

Range	S	AP	Type
-	4	5	Bomb 1, Large Blast, One use only

BOOM BOMB

Hurled into the foe using a Blitza-bommer's momentum, boom bombs can be deadly weapons providing the aircraft deploying them doesn't come to grief in the process.

Range	S	AP	Type
-	7	2	Bomb 1, Armourbane, Large Blast, Skreamin' Descent, One use only

Skreamin' Descent: Roll 2D6 and refer to the table below when making a Bombing Run attack with a Boom Bomb. The roll is made after the Blast marker is placed but before it scatters.

2D6	Result
2	**Faster! Waaagh! Uh oh**... No bomb is dropped. The flyer making the attack is wrecked and suffers a Crash and Burn result, with the large blast marker centred on the position occupied by the target model – the marker then scatters 2D6" as described in the Crash and Burn rule (see *Warhammer 40,000: The Rules*).
3	**Clipped 'im!** No bomb is dropped. The flyer making the attack and its target each suffer a single Strength 9 AP2 hit. All hits on vehicles strike the vehicle's side facing.
4-9	**Just like dis!** Execute the Bombing Run attack normally.
10-12	**Dakka-dakka-boom!** Execute the Bombing Run attack normally. In addition, the flyer making the attack may shoot any of its assault weapons at the target model's unit. All hits on vehicles strike the vehicle's rear facing. Any unit that suffers one or more unsaved Wounds from any of the attacks must take a Pinning test. Note that the flyer may shoot its assault weapons again in the Shooting phase and it can target a different unit.

FLAMER WEAPONS

All the following weapons are Flamer weapons for the purposes of any special rules that interact with Flamer weapons as described in *Warhammer 40,000: The Rules*. Profiles for the weapons in this section are also listed in the reference section (pg 104).

BURNA BOMB

A burna bomb is a large metal canister with an internal fuse. They are filled to the gunwales with sloshing promethium and squig-oil, and detonate on impact to spread flaming death across a wide area.

Range	S	AP	Type
-	5	4	Bomb 1, Large Blast, Ignores Cover, One use only

BURNA

Burnas are long-necked cutting torches that can focus their fiery emissions into a concentrated, metal-slicing jet or a billowing cloud of white-hot flame.

When a model attacks with a burna, it can use either of the profiles below. It cannot use both profiles in the same turn.

Range	S	AP	Type
Template	4	5	Assault 1
-	User	3	Melee, Two-handed

SKORCHA

Beloved of Ork arsonists, the skorcha is a huge flamethrower that sprays a great gout of burning fuel over the target area. Skorchas are most commonly mounted to Ork vehicles, though some Meks have been known to build them into kombi-shootas as well.

Range	S	AP	Type
Template	5	4	Assault 1

SKORCHA MISSILE

Skorcha missiles are 'fire and ferget' weapons used by Burna-bommer pilots to flush enemy infantry out of cover. Their warheads explode in sprays of chemical flame that burns white hot and makes a mockery of the mightiest fortifications.

Range	S	AP	Type
24"	5	4	Heavy 1, Blast, Ignores Cover, One use only

BUBBLECHUKKA

The bubblechukka generates clusters of force field bubbles that vary wildly in size and solidity, some like large balls that hit with all the force of a backhand slap, whilst others float down like small soap bubbles and burst with the strength of Gork himself.

Range	S	AP	Type
36"	D6*	D6*	Heavy 1, Large Blast

* Roll once each Shooting phase to determine both the Strength and AP of the bubblechukka, after the target unit has been chosen. For example, if you rolled a 3, the shot would be resolved at Strength 3 AP3.

DAKKAGUN

Dakkaguns are large, hopper-fed machine guns that spew crude bullets in sawing arcs.

Range	S	AP	Type
18"	5	5	Assault 3

DEFF KANNON

Stompas mount enormous deff kannons, capable of destroying entire infantry formations in one glorious explosion.

Range	S	AP	Type
72"	10	1	Primary Weapon 1, Massive Blast

DEFFGUN

Deffguns are massive, kustom-built gun rigs. When fired, these weapons launch unpredictable barrages of rockets, bullets and blasts that can tear formations of enemy warriors to bloody shreds.

Range	S	AP	Type
48"	7	4	Heavy D3*

* Roll once each time a unit makes a shooting attack with deffguns to determine how many shots all of the unit's deffguns will fire, after the target unit has been chosen.

GROT BLASTA

Grots sometimes manage to buy themselves a run-down, second-hand, low-tech piece of junk that might just conceivably kill something if Gork and Mork are feeling generous.

Range	S	AP	Type
12"	3	-	Assault 1

GROTZOOKA

These funnel-shaped weapons launch anything from spare ammo to scrap and nails, engulfing their targets in clouds of shrapnel.

Range	S	AP	Type
18"	6	5	Heavy 2, Blast

KANNON

These are large bore artillery pieces, crude but effective weapons that fire anti-tank shells or fused frag rounds.

	Range	S	AP	Type
Frag	36"	4	5	Heavy 1, Blast
Shell	36"	8	3	Heavy 1

KILLKANNON

The killkannon is usually mounted on Battlewagon turrets. What these guns lack in accuracy and range, they more than compensate for in explosive punch and sheer, deafening noise.

Range	S	AP	Type
24"	7	3	Ordnance 1, Large Blast

KOMBI-WEAPONS

Kombi-weapons are made by crudely welding, nailing or tying two guns together to ensure maximum dakka at the opportune moment.

A model armed with a kombi-weapon can choose to fire either the primary shoota (pg 96), or the secondary weapon, which will be either a rokkit launcha (see below) or a skorcha (pg 94). The shoota can be fired every turn, but the secondary weapon can only be fired once per battle. You cannot fire both weapons in the same turn. Each kombi-weapon has only one secondary weapon.

KUSTOM MEGA-WEAPONS

A Mek's favourite gun often becomes his pet project, tinkered with until it boasts a profusion of worky gubbinz and zappy bits. On a good day, even the most portable of such guns can melt a hole through a Space Marine at twenty paces. The power of kustom mega-weapons comes at a price, of course, and an overheated weapon is likely to blow up. Yet the spectacular damage these weapons can cause is considered to more than make up the risk.

	Range	S	AP	Type
Kustom mega-slugga	12"	8	2	Pistol, Gets Hot
Kustom mega-blasta	24"	8	2	Assault 1, Gets Hot
Kustom mega-kannon	36"	8	2	Heavy 1, Blast, Gets Hot

LOBBA

Most Lobbas are large, noisy mortars that are typically mounted onto battlewagons.

Range	S	AP	Type
48"	5	5	Heavy 1, Barrage, Blast

ROKKIT LAUNCHA

Crude but easy to manufacture, the rokkit launcha is a stout stick with a simple trigger mechanism that allows the Ork at the 'safe' end to fire a dodgy-looking rokkit in the general direction of the enemy.

Range	S	AP	Type
24"	8	3	Assault 1

SHOKK ATTACK GUN

The shokk attack gun projects a narrow force field tunnel through the Warp. The entrance to this tunnel opens at the front of the gun and the exit point is created wherever the operator aims it. Herds of Snotlings – along with the odd squig – are hurled down this hellish tunnel. The nightmarish journey through the Warp drives the Snotlings into a frenzy, and they emerge scrabbling, clawing, biting and defecating uncontrollably. As the Mek does his best to aim at the exact location of enemy soldiers, the Warp-crazed Snotlings emerge not so much into the ranks of the foe as inside the foe themselves. This can cause havoc in a vehicle and catastrophic trauma in enemy troopers, making this one of the deadliest of Ork weapons.

To fire the shokk attack gun, roll 2D6 to determine its Strength after placing the template but before rolling the Scatter dice. If an 11 or any double is rolled for the gun's Strength, consult the chart below.

Range	S	AP	Type
60"	2D6	2	Ordnance 1, Large Blast

Roll Result

1,1 Boom! No shot is fired. Remove the Mek as a casualty.

2,2 Oops! The opponent may choose the target of the shokk attack gun this turn, and place the Large Blast marker. The target can be a unit on the same side as the Mek.

3,3 Gah! Resolve the shot upon the nearest unit to the target that is not locked in combat, be it friend or foe.

4,4 Sploosh! Resolve the attack upon the target, but use the small blast marker. Any hits are resolved at Strength 6 AP6.

5,5 Zoink! No shot is fired. Immediately place the Mek in base contact with the closest model or point on the target unit, and treat them as being locked in combat.

5,6 Bzzap! Only the model under the template hole is hit, but the shot is Strength 10.

6,6 Krakoom! When resolving this shot, the shokk attack gun has the Vortex special rule.

SHOOTA WEAPONS

Shootas are noisy, large-calibre machine guns. They vary wildly in size and design, from those carried by foot-slogging Boyz to long barrelled supa-shootas that are mounted on aircraft. Regardless of their particular design, all shootas are both deafening and deadly.

	Range	S	AP	Type
Shoota	18"	4	6	Assault 2
Big shoota	36"	5	5	Assault 3
Supa shoota	36"	6	4	Assault 3
Deffstorm mega-shoota	36"	6	4	Heavy 3D6

SLUGGA

This ugly and brutish handgun is perfectly designed for its ugly and brutish owner to kill his foes, either by shooting them through the face at point-blank range or by beating them to death with it.

Range	S	AP	Type
12"	4	6	Pistol

SMASHA GUN

Based on lifta-droppa technology, this weapon traps its target in a localised force field. It then hoists them aloft and, with horrible finality, crushes them like a massive invisible fist. Of course, some targets are simply jerked skyward before dropping back to earth.

Range	S	AP	Type
36"	D6+4*	1	Heavy 1

* Roll once each Shooting phase to determine the Strength of the weapon, after the target unit has been chosen.

SNAZZGUN

Snazzguns are marvels of Orky know-wotz. Their owners pour countless teef into having additional barrels, drum magazines, and all manner of widgets and gubbinz attached to their prized guns. The resultant weapons have been known to fire clouds of flaming bullets, blasts of plasma or volleys of rocket-propelled grenades.

Range	S	AP	Type
24"	5	D6*	Assault 3

* Roll once each time the unit shoots to determine the AP of all the unit's snazzguns, after the target unit has been chosen.

SUPA-GATLER

Stompas mount a huge gatling cannon that fires a stream of high-calibre shells at an astonishing rate, scything through light vehicle squadrons and enemy infantry squads in seconds.

Range	S	AP	Type
48"	7	3	Heavy 2D6, Psycho-Dakka-Blasta!, Whirrrr Click-click

Psycho-Dakka-Blasta! The supa-gatler makes three shooting attacks with the profile above each time it fires. Completely resolve each shooting attack before moving onto the next. A new target may be chosen for each attack.

Whirrrr Click-click: If a double is rolled when determining the number of shots for any of the supa-gatler's shooting attacks, then it runs out of ammunition after that attack has been resolved, and cannot shoot again for the rest of the battle. This rule does not apply to the very first shooting attack a supa-gatler makes in a battle (so it will fire a minimum of two times before running out of ammunition).

SUPA-ROKKIT

It is a rare Stompa indeed that marches to war without several of these giant and highly unstable missiles bolted to its hull. When fired, they corkscrew wildly across the battlefield on a streamer of fire before ploughing into the foe's lines like the stomping foot of an angry Ork god.

Range	S	AP	Type
Infinite	8	3	Heavy 1, Large Blast, One use only

TELLYPORT BLASTA

The tellyport blasta folds its target in a Warpspace bubble and displaces it at random. Victims will only travel a short distance before they reappear, but this is sufficient to rematerialise them high in the air, or inside a solid object. Meks never know exactly what a tellyport blasta will do to its targets, but can be sure that the results will always be entertaining.

Range	S	AP	Type
12"	8	2	Assault 1, Blast, Tellyported

Tellyported: Any To Wound roll of a 6 made with this weapon has the Instant Death special rule. If this weapon rolls a 6 for armour penetration, it causes a penetrating hit, regardless of whether the armour penetration result was higher than the target's armour value or not.

TRAKTOR KANNON

The traktor kannon fires a thrumming beam of force high into the air. The grot crew swing this beam about wildly until they manage to latch the humming column onto an airborne target. Once snagged, their hapless victim is wrenched out of the air and smashed to bits on the ground below.

Range	S	AP	Type
36"	8	3	Heavy 1, Skyfire, Traktor

Traktor: This weapon automatically causes an Immobilised result in addition to any other effects when it scores a glancing or penetrating hit against a Zooming Flyer. If a Swooping Flying Monstrous Creature suffers one or more Wounds from this weapon it suffers a -3 penalty to its Grounded test that turn.

ZZAP GUN

Zzap guns fire unstable bolts of lightning. They have the potential to punch through the hull of even the heaviest enemy vehicle amid crackling showers of sparks, but have a tendency to overload and electrocute the operating gunner.

Range	S	AP	Type
36"	2D6	2	Heavy 1, Zzap, Gets Hot

Zzap: Each time a Zzap gun is fired, roll 2D6 to determine its Strength, after the target unit has been chosen. If the roll is above 10, the shot is resolved at Strength 10 and the weapon Gets Hot on any To Hit roll of 1, 2 or 3. If a Zzap gun Gets Hot, the Wound is resolved against the crew. Zzap guns automatically cause a Crew Shaken result in addition to any other effects when they score a glancing or penetrating hit.

RUNTS & SQUIGS

Runts and squigs are upgrades that may be taken by certain models in an Ork army. The upgrade is either represented on the model itself, or by a suitable model placed beside the model with the upgrade. Runt and squig models are purely decorative and are always ignored for game purposes – just move them to one side if they get in the way. If the runt or squig model represents a one use only effect, remove the model once it has been used.

AMMO RUNT

An ammo runt is a heavily overburdened Gretchin who carries extra ammunition for his master.

One use only. A model with an ammo runt can re-roll one To Hit roll when shooting.

ATTACK SQUIG

An attack squig is a voracious predator with a huge snapping gob.

A model with an attack squig is allowed to re-roll one To Hit roll in close combat each turn.

BOMB SQUIG

Bomb squigs will chase after anything that moves, and enterprising Tankbustas take advantage of this by strapping them with contact-mines and explosives before loosing them toward the enemy's tanks.

One use only. A model with a bomb squig can make a Shooting attack using the following profile. Bomb squigs cannot be used to make Snap Shots, and cannot be used to attack Flyers, Flying Monstrous Creatures, or Skimmers.

Range	S	AP	Type
18"	8	4	Assault 1, Scuttle Scuttle Blam!, One use only

Scuttle Scuttle Blam!: Bomb squigs always hit the target on a To Hit roll of 2 or more.

GROT OILER

Grot oilers are the assistants of Ork Meks, and are mostly employed putting out fires or crawling into functioning machinery.

One use only. A grot oiler allows a Mek to re-roll a failed Mek's Tools repair roll.

GROT ORDERLY

Painboyz are often accompanied by grot orderlies, whose job it is to carry tools and gather up discarded limbs and organs.

One use only. A grot orderly allows a Painboy's unit to re-roll a single Feel No Pain roll.

SQUIG HOUND

These fierce squigs are trained to devour errant grots on command.

Each time a unit with a squig hound fails a Morale check it suffers D6 Strength 3 AP- hits and must then re-roll the failed Morale check. If the re-roll is failed, it cannot be re-rolled again, and the squig hound will not inflict any further hits.

ORKY KNOW-WOTS

Rules for the following grenades can be found in *Warhammer 40,000: The Rules*:

Stikkbombs* Tankbusta bombs**
* See assault grenades ** See melta bombs

BOSSPOLE
Ork Nobz often sport a trophy pole that shows they are not to be messed with. A Nob with a Bosspole often finds it comes in handy when cracking heads to restore some order in the heat of battle.

Each time a unit that includes at least one model with a Bosspole rolls on the Mob Rule table (pg 92), you may choose to re-roll any result other than a Breaking Heads result. You must accept the result of the re-roll.

CYBORK BODY
Ork physiology is so robust that it can accept even the crudest cybernetics, whether the recipient asked the Dok to install it or not!

A model with a cybork body has the Feel No Pain (6+) special rule.

DOK'S TOOLS
From chain-scalpels and cranial trowels to a nicely weighted mallet, Ork surgical implements are crude yet surprisingly effective.

As long as the bearer is alive, all models in his unit have the Feel No Pain special rule.

GITFINDA
These can be elaborate ocular bionics, monocular head-sets, oversized telescopes, or Mork knows what else. The function of a gitfinda is to improve the accuracy of its user to near-average levels.

A model with a gitfinda that remained stationary during its Movement phase has Ballistic Skill 3 until the end of its turn.

KUSTOM FORCE FIELD
These bizarre devices are powered by crackling energy-coils and project invisible bubbles of energy that shield nearby Orks from incoming fire.

The bearer, and all models within 6", receive a 5+ invulnerable save against any shooting attacks. If the bearer is embarked in a vehicle, then the vehicle receives a 5+ invulnerable save against any shooting attacks instead.

MEK'S TOOLS
When going into battle, most Meks will bring with them a selection of their current favourites, inevitably including a nice, big wrench.

In each of your Shooting phases, instead of firing his weapons, a model equipped with Mek's tools may choose to repair a single friendly vehicle that he is in base contact with or embarked upon. To repair a vehicle, roll a D6. If the result is 5 or more, you may either restore a Hull Point lost earlier in the battle or repair a Weapon Destroyed result or an Immobilised result instead; this is effective immediately.

ROKKIT PACK
Stormboyz use crude rokkit packs to propel themselves across the battlefield in huge, bounding leaps. Whether they smash into enemy lines or a solid ferrocrete wall is a different matter entirely, however.

Models equipped with rokkit packs gain the Jump unit type as described in *Warhammer 40,000: The Rules*. A unit made up exclusively of models with rokkit packs can choose to use them to Run 2D6" in the Shooting phase instead of the normal D6", even if it used them in the Movement phase. If it does so, every model in the unit must take a Dangerous Terrain test.

WAAAGH! BANNER
A warband's banner is decorated with glyphs and trophies to show how dangerous the owners are. It is carried by a Nob who has earned his Warboss' respect. The banner has a near-religious significance to the Orks and they will fight all the harder in its presence.

All models in a unit that includes a Waaagh! Banner add +1 to the Weapon Skill characteristic on their profile.

WARBIKE
Orks love speed, really big guns, and making loads of noise. The warbike caters to all of these needs, with some extra speed to spare. Furthermore, when Warbikers open up their vehicles throttles they produce great clouds of smoky exhaust fumes, obscuring them from enemy fire.

A model equipped with a warbike changes their unit type to Bike, as described in *Warhammer 40,000: The Rules*. In addition, they have a 4+ Armour Save. Furthermore, if a model on a warbike turbo-boosts, it counts its cover save as being 1 point higher than normal until the start of its next turn. Warbikes are fitted with a twin-linked dakkagun.

Armour

'Eavy Armour

Ork 'eavy armour is hammered out of scrap iron, sheet metal and the looted battle-plate of fallen foes. Though its fit is dubious, 'eavy armour provides a solid defence for its wearer.

'Eavy armour confers a 4+ Armour Save.

Mega Armour

This is a suit of massively thick armour plates over a powered exoskeleton. Though seriously cumbersome, mega armour is the next best thing to getting wired into a Deff Dread, and renders its wearer impressively strong and hard to kill.

Mega armour confers a 2+ Armour Save. Models with mega armour have the Bulky and Slow and Purposeful special rules.

Ork Vehicle Equipment

> **Rules for the following upgrade can be found in Warhammer 40,000: The Rules:**
>
> Extra armour

'Ard Case

An armoured roof increases a wagon's survivability... a bit.

A vehicle with an 'ard case no longer counts as Open-topped. Note that this affects its Access Points and Fire Points as detailed in the appropriate datasheet entry.

Boarding Plank

Many Ork vehicles are fitted with a big metal boarding plank, often hinged and sporting spikes or hooks. This helps the Boyz to start piling out while their ride is still on the move.

If a unit disembarks from an Open-topped vehicle with a boarding plank and declares a charge in the same turn, it adds +2 to its charge distance (to a maximum of 12).

Deff Rolla

A deff rolla is a great spiked roller that brings the colossal weight of the Battlewagon to bear on anything in its way.

A vehicle with a deff rolla treats its front armour as two higher than normal when Ramming. In addition, if an enemy unit makes a Death or Glory attack on a vehicle with a deff rolla and fails to stop it, then the unit suffers D3 Strength 10 AP4 hits in addition to the damage they normally suffer for the failed attack. Furthermore, a vehicle with a deff rolla can re-roll failed Dangerous Terrain tests.

Grabbin' Klaw

Mounted on a pivoting crane arm and controlled by a number of kunnin' levers, a grabbin' klaw latches on to enemy tanks to prevent them 'runnin' away'.

At the beginning of the enemy Movement phase, nominate a single enemy vehicle that is within 2" of the vehicle's grabbin' klaw. On the roll of a 4+, that vehicle may not move this turn. Flyers and Skimmers cannot be attacked by a grabbin' klaw.

Flyboss

Flybosses are ace pilots who have survived more dogfights than they can count (even when using their toes).

A vehicle with a Flyboss has Ballistic Skill 3 when shooting at Jetbikes, Skimmers, Flyers or Flying Monstrous Creatures.

Grot Riggers

Whether hurriedly re-attaching gubbinz with rivet guns, or just getting out and pushing, a crew of grot riggers can help to keep an Ork vehicle in the fight long after it should have fallen apart.

A vehicle with grot riggers has the It Will Not Die special rule.

Red Paint Job

Orks believe that a vehicle painted red can outstrip a similar vehicle that isn't. As odd as it may seem, they're not wrong.

Ork vehicles with red paint jobs add +1" to their move when they move Flat Out.

Reinforced Ram

A vehicle fitted with such a blunt but effective ram can plough through wreckage, walls and enemy vehicles with equal ease.

A vehicle with a reinforced ram can Tank Shock and Ram, and treats its front Armour Value as two higher than normal when Ramming. Furthermore, the vehicle may re-roll failed Dangerous Terrain tests.

Stikkbomb Chukka

A stikkbomb chukka is a crude mechanism that lobs volleys of stikkbombs into the midst of the foe.

The vehicle is armed with stikkbombs. Any unit disembarking from a vehicle with a stikkbomb chukka is treated as having stikkbombs for the remainder of that turn.

Wreckin' Ball

Orks love demolition almost as much as they love war. The spiked wreckin' balls they mount on their vehicles fulfil both desires at once.

Range	S	AP	Type
3"	9	4	Assault D3

GIFTS OF GORK AND MORK

Gifts of Gork and Mork are items of such value and importance that entire tribes will go to war just to possess them. Believed by some to have been given to the Ork race by their careless, warring gods, each is unique. Only one of each of the following artefacts may be chosen per army – there is only one of each of these items in the galaxy!

DA FINKIN' KAP

Looted from a Schola Progenium training facility, this tangle of electrodes was incorporated into a helmet on the orders of Blood Axe Warboss Morgog. Upon donning the headgear, Morgog was bombarded by fragments of what he realised were strategies and tactics; though the crackling humie voices and flashes of imagery were confusing, the Warboss was able to make use of the concepts his new Finkin' Kap imparted. Soon his foes would learn that the only thing more dangerous than a savage three hundred pound brute is a savage three hundred pound brute with a plan.

The wearer of Da Finkin' Kap generates an additional Warlord Trait from the Strategic Traits table in *Warhammer 40,000: The Rules*. If the additional trait is the same as the first trait they generated, roll again until a different trait is generated.

WARBOSS GAZBAG'S BLITZBIKE

Originally owned by notorious Speed Freek Warboss Gazbag, this bike is an absolute monster. Although repeatedly stolen, patched up, kustomised and sold on, the warbike's core is the same. Its hugely overcharged engines and energy-shooting kustom dakkablastas render its rider a force of deadly destruction.

A model equipped with Warboss Gazbag's Blitzbike changes their unit type to Bike, as described in *Warhammer 40,000: The Rules*. In addition, this model has a 4+ Armour Save. When turbo-boosting, this model can move up to 18" instead of 12" and counts its cover save as being 1 point higher than normal until the start of its next turn. Warboss Gazbag's Blitzbike is equipped with twin-linked kustom dakkablastas with the following profile:

Range	S	AP	Type
24"	6	3	Assault 3

DA LUCKY STIKK

Makari was an exceptionally lucky grot who survived to the ripe old age of nine before finally meeting his end under the posterior of his hulking master. The plucky grot served as self-appointed banner-waver to the mighty Ghazghkull Thraka himself, surviving countless battles in ever more improbable ways. Ghazghkull saw Makari as something of a mascot. Thus, when the grot's remains were peeled off his boss' rear end, Makari's wavin' stikk was reclaimed, hosed down, and went into service as an impressive bosspole. Good fortune still surrounds Da Lucky Stikk, though the backlash when things go wrong can be surprisingly brutal.

All models in the bearer's unit add +1 to the Weapon Skill characteristic on their profile (this is not cumulative with the bonus from a Waaagh! banner). In addition, the bearer can choose to re-roll any failed To Hit or To Wound rolls or saving throws that they make. However, should three or more of the re-rolls generate failed results in the same turn, the model is immediately removed as a casualty with no saving throws of any kind allowed.

HEADWOPPA'S KILLCHOPPA

Grand Warboss Headwoppa had a real thing for decapitating his enemies. Whenever the Warboss lopped the head from an opponent, his ladz would raise a raucous cheer. Headwoppa and his tribe were last seen charging headlong into a horde of Khornate Daemons at the heart of the Vandengheist Nebula. Yet legend speaks of a blood-slick big choppa that still turns up occasionally. Though this weapon looks normal, a dark voice is said to growl into the mind of its wielder, driving him on to ever greater excesses of bloodthirsty violence.

Range	S	AP	Type
-	+2	5	Melee, Decapitating Strike, Rending, Two-handed

Decapitating Strike: Any To Wound roll of a 6 made with Headwoppa's Killchoppa has the Instant Death special rule.

DA FIXER UPPERZ

Originally the tools of Mekaniak Frazdak, it is claimed that da Fixer Upperz can repair any wagon, no matter how badly junked it might appear. In typically Orky fashion, the sheer belief that these tools can work wonders often seems to mean they do just that!

In each of your Shooting phases, instead of firing a weapon, a model equipped with da Fixer Upperz can choose to repair a single friendly vehicle he is in base contact with or embarked upon. To repair a vehicle, roll a D6. If the result is 3 or more, you may either restore a lost Hull Point or repair a Weapon Destroyed or an Immobilised result instead; this is effective immediately.

DA DEAD SHINY SHOOTA

Rumoured to have been made by Bigmek Buzzgob, da Dead Shiny Shoota is a double-barrelled brute packed full of dakka. Bought and sold for piles of teef, or prised from the dead hands of its previous owner, this shoota has found its way into numerous tribes in its lifetime. The gun kicks out a deafening storm of hot lead, much to the enjoyment of the Ork pulling the trigger. Of course with so much firepower, the odd round finds its way into an Ork, also much to the amusement of the shooter.

Range	S	AP	Type
18"	4	6	Assault 6, Stray Shot, Twin-linked

Stray Shot: Roll a D6 each time da Dead Shiny Shoota fails To Hit its target (after re-rolls). For each roll of 1, a friendly unit within 6" of the target, chosen by your opponent, suffers a single Strength 4 AP6 hit as if it were just shot by the wielder of da Dead Shiny Shoota. The wielder of da Dead Shiny Shoota, and his unit, cannot be chosen as the targets for a Stray Shot.

THE POWER OF THE WAAAGH!

Ork Weirdboyz have no choice in the use of their psychic abilities. When the Waaagh! energy is flowing, they helplessly absorb wave after wave of power until every fibre of their being is suffused with it. Weirdboyz must either vent this power in great roaring blasts, or else suffer a messy and explosive death as the Waaagh! energy creates an exit of its own!

PRIMARIS POWER

FRAZZLE .... WARP CHARGE 1

The Weirdboy sends out arcs of crackling psychic energy that ground themselves upon the enemy, reducing them to shrivelled husks before the eyes of their terrified comrades.

Frazzle is a **witchfire** power with the following profile:

Range	S	AP	Type
24"	6	3	Assault 1, Blast

1. 'EADBANGER .... WARP CHARGE 1

A violent bolt of power erupts from the Weirdboy's sloping forehead and rockets across the battlefield, causing the head of the first unfortunate victim caught in its path to explode in a shower of brains and gore.

'Eadbanger is a **focussed witchfire** power with a range of 24". The target must pass a Toughness test or suffer a Wound with no armour or cover saves allowed.

2. WARPATH .... WARP CHARGE 1

The Weirdboy disperses the Waaagh! energy coursing through his frame into the Ork warriors around him, stirring their already bellicose, warlike nature to roaring fever pitch.

Warpath is a **blessing** that targets the Psyker. Whilst the power is in effect, all models in the Psyker's unit that have the 'Ere We Go special rule gain +1 Attack.

3. DA JUMP .... WARP CHARGE 1

The Weirdboy closes his eyes tight and, in a storm of flashing green light, teleports himself to another part of the battlefield – along with any confused Boyz who happened to be standing too close to him at the time.

Da Jump is a **blessing** that targets the Psyker and his unit. Remove the unit from the board. It then immediately arrives using the rules for Deep Strike anywhere on the battlefield. If the deep striking unit scatters and a double is rolled, the unit can only make Snap Shots until the start of its next turn.

4. KILLBOLT .... WARP CHARGE 2

A crackling surge of Waaagh! energy lances forth from the Weirdboy's eyesockets – anything in its path is reduced to a pile of glowing green embers.

Killbolt is a **beam** with the following profile:

Range	S	AP	Type
18"	10	2	Assault 1

5. POWER VOMIT .... WARP CHARGE 2

Fanged maw yawning wide, the Weirdboy vomits a roiling tide of searing green psycho-plasma from his churning innards that burns through everything in its path, leaving nothing but scorched earth and fluorescent embers in its wake.

Power Vomit is a **witchfire** power with the following profile:

Range	S	AP	Type
Template	7	2	Assault 1

6. DA KRUNCH .... WARP CHARGE 2

The Weirdboy's fevered brain conjures a huge ectoplasmic vision of either a giant, warty green fist or foot that pummels the foe into a mushy paste.

Da Krunch is a **witchfire** power with the following profile:

Range	S	AP	Type
24"	2D6*	4	Assault 1, Large Blast, Barrage

* If, when rolling to determine *Da Krunch*'s Strength, you roll an 11 or 12, completely resolve the attack at Strength 10 and then roll another 2D6 and resolve a second attack against the original target of the psychic power (if it still has any surviving models). If this second attack also rolls an 11 or 12 for its Strength, resolve another attack as described above. Continue repeating this process until either you roll a 10 or less when determining the attack's Strength, or the original target is completely destroyed.

OLD ZOGWORT

Born during a total eclipse amid a nest of bloodvipers, the young Zogwart fought his way to safety, suffering dozens of venomous bites yet biting back in return. He survived, and from that day on was revered by his tribe. Vipers infested Zogwart's clothes, and his bite was soon as venomous as theirs. Yet Zogwort's most potent power was his infamous curse that would engulf foes in a blinding green light before transforming them into puzzled-looking squigs. Eventually, Zogwort became so powerful that a vast retinue gathered around him, a Waaagh! that the maddened Warphead leads on a wild rampage through the stars.

ORK HORDE DETACHMENT

Codex: Orks details a unique Detachment – the Ork Horde Detachment – that reflects the horde-like nature of the greenskins. This follows all the Detachment rules presented in *Warhammer 40,000: The Rules*.

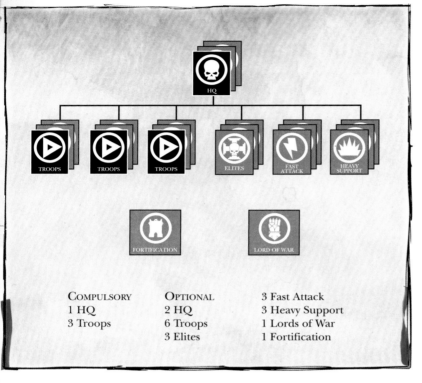

COMPULSORY	OPTIONAL	
1 HQ	2 HQ	3 Fast Attack
3 Troops	6 Troops	3 Heavy Support
	3 Elites	1 Lords of War
		1 Fortification

RESTRICTIONS

All units in this Detachment must have the Orks Faction (or have no Faction).

COMMAND BENEFITS

Boss of Da Waaagh!: If this Detachment is chosen as your Primary Detachment, you can re-roll the result when rolling on the Warlord Traits table in *Codex: Orks*.

The Greenskin Hordes: Every unit with 10 or more models in this Detachment gains the Hammer of Wrath special rule in any Assault phase in which it successfully charges an enemy unit and the dice rolled for its charge range is 10 or more (before modifiers). Note that the unit does not need to move the full distance rolled to gain this effect and it does not matter if the unit's size is reduced below 10 models during its charge (as a result of Overwatch, Dangerous Terrain tests etc.) so long as it can still successfully make the charge.

ORK TACTICAL OBJECTIVES

Codex: Orks describes six Tactical Objectives to use in your games that are exclusive to greenskin players and help to reflect their brutal yet kunnin' method of war.

If your Warlord has the Orks Faction, these Tactical Objectives replace the Capture & Control Tactical Objectives (numbers 11-16) described in *Warhammer 40,000: The Rules*.

If a Warhammer 40,000 mission has the Tactical Objectives special rule, players use the normal rules for using Tactical Objectives (see *Warhammer 40,000: The Rules*) with the following exception: when an Ork player generates a Capture & Control objective (numbers 11, 12, 13, 14, 15 or 16), the Ork player instead generates the corresponding Ork Tactical Objective, as shown in the table opposite.

Other Tactical Objectives (numbers 21-66) are generated normally, as described in *Warhammer 40,000: The Rules*.

D66	RESULT
11	More Dakka!
12	Get 'em, Boss!
13	Stomp 'em, Boyz!
14	More Speed, Go Fasta!
15	Grab da Loot!
16	'Ere We Go! WAAAGH!

---

11 MORE DAKKA!
TYPE: ORKS
Da only thing better than loads of dakka is even more dakka.

Score 1 Victory Point at the end of your turn if at least one enemy unit was completely destroyed during your Shooting phase.

12 GET 'EM BOSS!
TYPE: ORKS
You call dat fightin' you runty wimp? I'll show yer how it's done!

Score 1 Victory Point at the end of your turn if your Warlord killed an opponent in a challenge during your turn. If your Warlord killed the enemy's Warlord in a challenge during your turn, score D3 Victory points instead.

13 STOMP 'EM, BOYZ!
TYPE: ORKS
What are you lot waiting fer? Get stuck in and bash some heads!

Score 1 Victory Point at the end of your turn if at least one enemy unit was completely destroyed during your Assault phase. If 3 to 5 enemy units were completely destroyed during your Assault phase, score D3 Victory Points instead. If 6 or more enemy units were completely destroyed during your Assault phase, score D3+3 Victory Points instead.

14 MORE SPEED, GO FASTA!
TYPE: ORKS
Hurry up! Get a move on you'll miss da best of the fightin'.

Score 1 Victory Point at the end of your turn if at least three Ork units Turbo-boosted, went Flat Out or Ran 6" or more during your turn.

15 GRAB DA LOOT!
TYPE: ORKS
There's loads of gubbinz to loot, but if you don't get it soon some other thievin' git will nick it.

Roll a D6 when this Tactical Objective is generated. Score 1 Victory Point at the end of your turn if you control the Objective Marker whose number corresponds to the D6 result.

16 'ERE WE GO! WAAAGH!
TYPE: ORKS
Time to show this cowardly bunch of pansies that Orks is da best. Waaagh!

Score 1 Victory Point at the end of your turn if, during that turn, you successfully charged an enemy unit with an Ork unit and the dice rolled for its charge distance was 10 or more (before modifiers). If, during your turn, 3 or more Ork units did this, score D3 Victory Points instead. Note that the Ork units do not need to move the full distance rolled to score this Tactical Objective.

DESIGNER'S NOTE –
TACTICAL OBJECTIVES CARD DECK
If you own a deck of Ork Tactical Objective Cards, you can generate your Tactical Objectives by shuffling the deck and drawing the top card instead of rolling a D66. These should be kept face up, so your opponent can see which Tactical Objectives you have generated, unless the mission you are playing instructs you otherwise.

REFERENCE

ARMY SPECIAL RULES (PG 92)

'Ere We Go!: Re-roll a dice when determining charge range.

Mob Rule: If the unit fails a Morale or Pinning test, roll immediately on the following table:

D6	RESULT
1	**Born to Fight:** If the unit is locked in combat, it is treated as if it had passed the Morale or Pinning test. If not locked in combat, it fails the test.
2-3	**Breaking Heads:** If the unit includes one or more Ork characters, it suffers D6 Strength 4 AP- hits, and is treated as if it had passed the Morale or Pinning test. Hits are Randomly Allocated, but cannot be allocated to Ork characters (excess hits are lost). If the unit does not include any Ork characters, it fails the test.
4-6	**Squabble:** If the unit has 10 or more models, it suffers D6 Strength 4 AP- hits, and is treated as if it had passed the Morale or Pinning test. Hits are Randomly Allocated. If it has less than 10 models, it fails the test.

WARLORD TRAITS (PG 92)

D6	WARLORD TRAIT
1	**Prophet of the Waaagh!:** Warlord gains Waaagh! (pg 54). If the Warlord already has Waaagh! then all friendly units with 'Ere We Go! also gain Fearless when he calls a Waaagh!, until the start of the next friendly turn.
2	**Bellowing Tyrant:** Warlord and all friendly units with the Orks Faction within 12" of him re-roll failed Morale and Pinning tests.
3	**Like a Thunderbolt!:** Warlord and all friendly units with the Orks Faction within 12" of him can re-roll all the dice when determining Run moves or charge range.
4	**Brutal but Kunnin':** Warlord can re-roll one failed To Hit or To Wound roll each turn.
5	**Kunnin' but Brutal:** Warlord can re-roll one failed armour or invulnerable saving throw each turn.
6	**Might is Right:** Warlord has +1 Strength.

RUNTS & SQUIGS (PG 97)

Ammo runt: One use only. A model with an ammo runt can re-roll one To Hit roll when shooting.

Attack squig: Re-roll one To Hit roll in close combat each turn.

Bomb squig: Shooting attack using the following profile. Cannot be used to make Snap Shots. Cannot be used to attack Flyers, Flying Monstrous Creatures, or Skimmers.

Range	S	AP	Type
18"	8	4	Assault 1, Scuttle Scuttle Blam!, One use only

Scuttle Scuttle Blam!: Always hits on a 2+.

Grot oiler: Re-roll a single failed Mek's tools repair roll. Remove the oiler model once he has been used.

Grot orderly: Re-roll a single Feel No Pain roll. Remove the grot orderly model once he has been used.

Squig hound: If a unit fails a Morale check it suffers D6 Strength 3 AP- hits and must re-roll. If the re-roll is failed, it cannot be re-rolled again, and the squig hound will not inflict any hits.

ARMOUR (PG 99)

'Eavy Armour: 4+ Armour Save.

Mega Armour: 2+ Armour Save, Bulky, Slow and Purposeful.

HQ

	WS	BS	S	T	W	I	A	Ld	Sv	Unit Type	Pg
	4	2	4	4	2	3	3	8	6+	In (ch)	57
k	5	2	5	4	2	3	4	8	4+	In, J (ch)	61
ukk	5	2	4	4	2	3	4	9	3+	In (ch)	60
rotsnik	5	2	4	5	3	3	4	9	4+	In (ch)	59
	4	2	3	4	1	2	2	7	6+	In (ch)	56
	4	2	4	4	2	3	3	7	6+	In (ch)	58
	5	2	5	5	3	4	4	9	6+	In (ch)	54
	4	2	4	4	2	3	3	7	6+	In (ch)	55

TROOPS

	WS	BS	S	T	W	I	A	Ld	Sv	Unit Type	Pg
	4	2	4	4	2	3	3	7	6+	In (ch)	62
	2	3	2	2	1	2	1	5	-	In	63
	4	2	3	4	1	2	2	7	6+	In	62
	4	2	3	4	1	2	2	7	6+	In (ch)	63

ELITES

	WS	BS	S	T	W	I	A	Ld	Sv	Unit Type	Pg
ganob	4	2	4	4	2	3	3	7	2+	In (ch)	67
	4	2	4	4	2	3	3	7	6+	In (ch)	var
krot	5	2	5	4	2	3	4	8	6+	In (ch)	69
oy	4	2	3	4	1	2	2	7	6+	In	64
ndo	4	2	3	4	1	2	2	7	6+	In	68
b	4	2	4	4	2	3	3	7	2+	In (ch)	67
	4	2	3	4	1	2	2	7	6+	In (ch)	64
	4	2	4	4	2	3	3	7	6+	In	66
sta	4	2	3	4	1	2	2	7	6+	In	65

FAST ATTACK

	WS	BS	S	T	W	I	A	Ld	Sv	Unit Type	Pg
ob	4	2	4	4	2	3	3	7	6+	In, J (ch)	71
ob (Warbiker)	4	2	4	5	2	3	3	7	4+	Bk (ch)	76
pta	4	2	3	5	2	2	2	7	4+	Jb	72
boy	4	2	3	4	1	2	2	7	6+	In, J	71
ker	4	2	3	5	1	2	2	7	4+	Bk	76

HEAVY SUPPORT

	WS	BS	S	T	W	I	A	Ld	Sv	Unit Type	Pg
Gun	-	-	-	7	2	-	-	-	3+	Ar	78
Git	4	2	4	4	2	3	3	7	6+	In	85
hin	2	3	2	2	1	2	1	5	-	Ar	78
in	4	2	4	4	2	3	3	7	6+	In (ch)	85
a	4	2	3	4	1	2	2	7	6+	In	84
	4	2	3	4	1	2	2	7	6+	In (ch)	84

LORDS OF WAR

	WS	BS	S	T	W	I	A	Ld	Sv	Unit Type	Pg
azghkull Thraka	6	2	5	5	4	4	5	9	2+	In (ch)	86

VEHICLES

	WS	BS	S	F	S	R	I	A	HP	Unit Type	Pg
ttlewagon		2		14	12	10			4	Tk, O, T	79
rna-bommer		2		10	10	10			3	Fl	74
itza-bommer		2		10	10	10			3	Fl	75
akkajet		2		10	10	10			3	Fl	73
eff Dread	4	2	5	12	12	10	2	3	3	W	80
orkanaut	4	2	8	13	13	12	2	4	5	W, T	82
illa Kan	2	3	5	11	11	10	2	2	2	W	81
Morkanaut	4	2	8	13	13	12	2	4	5	W, T	83
korcha		2		10	10	10			2	F, O	77
tompa	4	2	10	13	13	12	1	4	12	ShW, T	87
rukk		2		10	10	10			3	F, O, T	70
Warbuggy		2		10	10	10			2	F, O	77
Wartrakk		2		10	10	10			2	F, O	77

WEAPONS

Weapon	Range	S	AP	Type
Big choppa	-	+2	5	Melee, Two-handed
Big shoota	36"	5	5	Assault 3
Bigbomm	-	4	5	Bomb 1, Large Blast, One use only
Bomb squig	18"	8	4	Assault 1, Bomb Squig, One use only
Boom bomb	-	7	2	Bomb 1, Armourbane, Large Blast, Skreamin' Descent, One use only
Bubblechukka	36"	D6	D6	Heavy 1, Large Blast
Burna (close combat)	-	User	3	Melee, Two-handed
Burna (shooting)	Template	4	5	Assault 1
Burna bomb	-	5	4	Bomb 1, Large Blast, Ignores Cover, One use only
Buzzsaw	-	x2	2	Melee, Unwieldy, Specialist Weapon
Choppa	-	User	-	Melee
Close combat weapon	-	User	-	Melee
Dakkagun	18"	5	5	Assault 3
Deff kannon	72"	10	1	Primary Weapon 1, Massive Blast
Deffgun	48"	7	4	Heavy D3
Deffstorm mega-shoota	36"	5	5	Heavy 3D6
Grabba stikk	-	User	-	Melee, Throttle
Grot blasta	12"	3	-	Assault 1
Grot-prod	-	User	-	Melee, High Voltage
Grotzooka	18"	6	5	Heavy 2, Blast
Kannon				
- Frag	36"	4	5	Heavy 1, Blast
- Shell	36"	8	3	Heavy 1
Kan klaw	-	+2	2	Melee
Killkannon	24"	7	3	Ordnance 1, Large Blast
Killsaw	-	x2	2	Melee, Armourbane, Specialist Weapon, Unwieldy
Klaw of Gork (or possibly Mork)	-	10	1	Melee, Concussive
Kustom mega-blasta	24"	8	2	Assault 1, Gets Hot
Kustom mega-kannon	36"	8	2	Heavy 1, Blast, Gets Hot
Kustom mega-slugga	12"	8	2	Pistol, Gets Hot
Lobba	48"	5	5	Heavy 1, Barrage, Blast
Mega-choppa	-	D	1	Melee
Power klaw	-	x2	2	Melee, Unwieldy, Specialist Weapon
Rokkit launcha	24"	8	3	Assault 1
Shokk attack gun	60"	2D6	2	Ordnance 1, Large Blast
Shoota	18"	4	6	Assault 2
Skorcha	Template	5	4	Assault 1
Skorcha missile	24"	5	4	Heavy 1, Blast, Ignores Cover, One use only
Slugga	12"	4	6	Pistol
Smasha gun	36"	D6+4	1	Heavy 1
Snazzgun	24"	5	D6	Assault 3
Stikkbombs	8"	3	-	Assault 1, Blast
Supa shoota	36"	6	4	Assault 3
Supa-gatler	48"	7	3	Heavy 2D6, Psycho-Dakka-Blasta!, Whirrrr Click-click
Supa-rokkit	Infinite	8	3	Heavy 1, Large Blast, One use only
Tankbusta bombs	-	8	1	Armourbane, Unwieldy
Tankhammer	-	8	3	Melee, Two-handed, Unwieldy
Tellyport blasta	12"	8	2	Assault 1, Blast, Tellyported
Traktor kannon	36"	8	3	Heavy 1, Skyfire, Traktor
'Urty syringe	-	User	-	Melee, Poisoned (4+)
Weirdboy staff	-	+2	4	Melee, Force, Two-handed
Wreckin' ball	3"	9	4	Assault D3
Zzap gun	36"	2D6	2	Heavy 1, Zzap, Gets Hot

UNIT TYPES

Artillery = Ar, *Bike* = Bk, *Fast* = F, *Flyer* = Fl, *Infantry* = In,
Jetbike = Jb, *Jump unit* = J, *Open-topped* = O,
Super-heavy Walker = ShW, *Tank* = Tk, *Transport* = T,
Walker = W, *Character* = (ch)

ORK VEHICLE EQUIPMENT (PG 99)

'Ard Case: No longer counts as Open-topped. This affects its Access and Fire Points as detailed in its datasheet entry.

Boarding Plank: If a unit disembarks from an Open-topped vehicle and declares a charge in the same turn, it adds +2 to its charge distance (to a maximum of 12).

Deff Rolla: Treats front armour as two higher than normal when Ramming. If an enemy unit makes a Death or Glory attack on the vehicle and fails to stop it, the unit suffers D3 Strength 10 AP4 hits in addition to the damage they suffer normally. Can re-roll Dangerous Terrain tests.

Flyboss: Ballistic Skill 3 when shooting at Jetbikes, Skimmers, Flyers or Flying Monstrous Creatures.

Grabbin' Klaw: At the beginning of the enemy Movement phase, nominate an enemy vehicle within 2" of the grabbin' klaw. On a 4+, that vehicle may not move this turn. Flyers and Skimmers cannot be attacked by a grabbin' klaw.

Grot Riggers: It Will Not Die.

Red Paint Job: Adds 1" to Flat Out moves.

Reinforced Ram: Can Tank Shock and Ram, and treats front armour as two higher than normal when Ramming. May re-roll Dangerous Terrain tests.

Stikkbomb Chukka: Vehicle has stikkbombs. Any unit disembarking is treated as having stikkbombs for the remainder of that turn.

Wreckin' Ball:

Range	S	AP	Type
3"	9	4	Assault D3

SPECIAL RULES

Cowardly Grots! (pg 81): If the unit suffers 25% or more casualties during a phase, roll a D6. Add +1 if there are three or more Killa Kans in the unit, and +1 if there are one or more Deff Dreads within 6". On a 3+ nothing happens. On a roll of 1-2 every model in the unit immediately suffers Crew Shaken. No models lose a Hull Point as a result.

Effigy (pg 87): All friendly units with the Ork Faction within 6" have Fearless.

Glory Hogs (pg 65): In a mission that has First Blood, the Ork player receives double the normal Victory Points if the first casualty is an enemy vehicle destroyed by attacks made by one or more units of Tankbustas.

Grot Gunner (pg 74): When firing a big shoota or twin-linked big shoota, shots are resolved at Ballistic Skill 3.

Mekaniaks (pg 56): You may take one of these models for each other HQ choice. They do not use up a Force Organisation chart slot. If possible, assign this model to a unit of Infantry of Artillery in its detachment before the game begins. It is part of that unit for the rest of the battle.

Ramshackle (pg 70): Roll a D6 when the vehicle suffers a penetrating hit. On a 6 that hit is a glancing hit instead.

Stampede (pg 89): If the Warboss is your Warlord he can use his Waaagh! special rule every turn after the first.

Trakked (pg 77): Re-rolls failed Dangerous Terrain tests.

Waaagh! (pg 54): Once per game, if the model is your Warlord, they can call a Waaagh! at the start of any of your turns after the first. That turn, all units made exclusively of models with 'Ere We Go! may declare a charge in the Assault phase even if they made a Run move.

Waaagh! Energy (pg 55): Generates +1 Warp Charge point if, at the start of your Psychic phase, there are ten or more models with the 'Ere We Go! special rule within 12". If he does so, he must pass at least one Psychic test that phase or suffer a single Strength 2 hit with no saves allowed. Does not apply if the Weirdboy is in a Transport or Building.

Waaagh! Plane (pg 73): During a turn in which a Waaagh! is called, each of this model's Assault weapons fires one more shot than normal.

ORKY KNOW-WOTS (PG 98)

Bosspole: Each time a unit that includes at least one model with a Bosspole rolls on the Mob Rule table (pg 92), you may choose to re-roll any result other than a Breaking Heads result. You must accept the result of the re-roll.

Cybork Body: Feel No Pain (6+).

Dok's Tools: As long as the bearer is alive, all models in his unit have Feel No Pain.

Gitfinda: A model that remained stationary during its Movement phase has Ballistic Skill 3 until the end of its turn.

Kustom Force Field: All models within 6" receive a 5+ invulnerable save against any shooting attack. If embarked in a vehicle, the vehicle receives a 5+ invulnerable save instead.

Mek's Tools: In your Shooting phase, instead of firing, this model can repair a friendly vehicle in base contact or that he is embarked upon. Roll a D6. If the result is 5+, restore a Hull Point or repair a Weapon Destroyed or Immobilised result.

Rokkit Pack: Unit type gains Jump. A unit made exclusively of models with rokkit packs can use them to Run 2D6" instead of D6" in the Shooting phase, even if it used them in the Movement phase. If it does so, every model must take a Dangerous Terrain test.

Stikkbombs: Assault grenades.

Tankbusta bombs: Melta bombs.

Waaagh! Banner: All models in the unit have +1 Weapon Skill.

Warbike: Unit type changes to Bike. Gains 4+ Armour Save and a twin-linked dakkagun. If the model turbo-boosts, they gain +1 cover save until the start of their next turn.

PSYCHIC POWERS (PG 101)

PRIMARIS POWER
FRAZZLE
Warp Charge 1. Witchfire.

Range	S	AP	Type
24"	6	3	Assault 1, Blast

1. 'EADBANGER
Warp Charge 1. Focussed Witchfire.
Range 24". Target must pass a Toughness test or suffer a Wound with no armour or cover saves allowed.

2. WARPATH
Warp Charge 1. Blessing.
Targets the Psyker. Whilst in effect, all models in the Psyker's unit with the 'Ere We Go special rule have +1 Attack.

3. DA JUMP
Warp Charge 1. Blessing.
Targets the Psyker and his unit. Remove the unit from the board. It then immediately Deep Strikes, anywhere on the battlefield. If the Deep Strike attempt scatters and a double is rolled, the unit can only make Snap Shots until the start of its next turn.

4. KILLBOLT
Warp Charge 2. Beam.

Range	S	AP	Type
18"	10	2	Assault 1

5. POWER VOMIT
Warp Charge 2. Witchfire.

Range	S	AP	Type
Template	7	2	Assault 1

6. DA KRUNCH
Warp Charge 2. Witchfire

Range	S	AP	Type
24"	2D6*	4	Assault 1, Large Blast, Barrage

* If you roll an 11 or 12 for Strength, resolve the attack at Strength 10 and then roll another 2D6 and resolve a second attack against the same target. If this attack rolls an 11 or 12, resolve another attack as described above. Repeat this process until you roll a 10 or less or the original target is destroyed.